THE REAL AND ITS DOUBLE

THE
SEAGULL
LIBRARY OF
FRENCH
LITERATURE

THE REAL AND ITS DOUBLE

CLÉMENT ROSSET

TRANSLATED BY CHRIS TURNER

LONDON NEW YORK CALCUTTA

Seagull Books, 2024

First published as *Le Réel et son double*: *Essai sur l'illusion*
by Clément Rosset, 1976

© Editions GALLIMARD, Paris, 1976 and 1985

First published in English translation by Seagull Books, 2012
Translation © Chris Turner, 2012

First published in paperback edition, 2024

ISBN 978 1 80309 523 3

British Library Cataloguing-in-Publication Data
A catalogue record for this book is available from the British Library

Typeset by Seagull Books, Calcutta, India
Printed and bound by WordsWorth India, New Delhi, India

CONTENTS

ILLUSION AND THE DOUBLE

I mean the way he has *'de nier ce qui
est et d'expliquer ce qui n'est pas.'*

Edgar Allan Poe
'The Murders in the Rue Morgue' (1841)

There is nothing more fragile than the human faculty
for consenting to reality, for accepting unreservedly the
imperious prerogative of the real. That faculty is so
often found wanting that it seems reasonable to imagine
it does not involve the recognition of an inalienable
right—the right of the real to be perceived—but represents a kind of conditional, provisional *tolerance*. A
tolerance anyone can suspend at will, as soon as the circumstances demand it, much as the customs authorities
may decide from one day to the next that the bottle of
spirits or 10 packs of cigarettes, which have up until now
been 'tolerated', will no longer be allowed through. If
travellers abuse the customs authorities' leniency, then

those authorities harden their attitude and refuse to let anything pass. Similarly, the real is admitted only on certain conditions and up to a point: if it abuses its rights and behaves disagreeably, the tolerance is suspended. An arresting of perception then shelters consciousness from any undesirable spectacle. As for the real, if it is absolutely insistent on being perceived, it can always darned well go and show itself *elsewhere*.

This refusal of the real may assume forms that are, naturally, very varied. Reality may be rejected radically, regarded purely and simply as non-being: 'this thing— which I believe I see—does not exist.' Moreover, the techniques available for such a radical negation are themselves very diverse. I can annihilate the real by annihilating myself. This is the formula of suicide, which appears the safest of all, even though a tiny coefficient of uncertainty still seems to attach to it, if we are to believe Hamlet:

> Who would fardels bear,
> To grunt and sweat under a weary life,
> But that the dread of something after death,
> The undiscover'd country from whose bourn
> No traveller returns, puzzles the will
> And makes us rather bear those ills we have
> Than fly to others that we know not of?[1]

I can also suppress the real at less cost to myself, sparing my life at the expense of mental collapse. This is the formula of madness. It, too, is a very certain method but it is not within everyone's grasp. As Henry

Ey's famous phrase has it, 'N'est pas fou qui veut'—one cannot become mad just by wishing to be. In exchange for the loss of my mental equilibrium, I shall obtain more or less effective protection from the real: a provisional distancing from it in the case of the *repression* described by Sigmund Freud (traces of the real persist in my Unconscious), its total eclipse in the *foreclosure* described by Jacques Lacan. I can, lastly, without sacrificing anything of either my life or my lucidity, decide not to see a real whose existence I do actually recognize. This is the attitude of voluntary blindness, symbolized by Oedipus' act of putting out his eyes at the end of *Oedipus Rex*, which finds more ordinary applications in the immoderate use of alcohol or drugs.

However, these radical forms of rejection of the real remain marginal and relatively exceptional. The commonest attitude in the face of unpleasant reality is rather different. If the real is a burden to me and I wish to free myself from it, I shall take a generally more flexible path towards ridding myself of it by way of a mode of reception that is located half-way between acceptance and pure and simple expulsion. A path that involves saying neither yes nor no to the thing perceived or, rather, saying both yes and no to it. Yes to the thing perceived, no to the consequences that ought normally to follow. This other way of being rid of the real resembles a correct line of reasoning that ends in an aberrant conclusion. It is an accurate perception that turns out to be incapable of issuing in behaviour adapted to that perception. In this case I do not refuse to see, nor do I in any way deny the real that is shown to me. But my consent stops there. I have seen something and accepted it but don't ask any more of me than that. In all other ways, I maintain my previous point of view, persist in my earlier behaviour, as though I had seen nothing. Paradoxically, my present perception and my earlier standpoint coexist. What we have here is a perception that is not so much erroneous as *useless*.

This 'useless perception' constitutes, it seems, one of the most remarkable characteristics of *illusion or delusion*. We would probably be wrong to regard these latter as arising principally out of a deficiency of sight. The deluded, it is sometimes said, do not see: they are blind or blinded. Reality may well offer itself up to their perception but they do not succeed in perceiving it, or perceive it in a distorted way, being so attentive as they are to the fantasies of their imagination and their desire. This analysis, which is without doubt valid where strictly clinical cases of refusal or absence of perception are concerned, seems very perfunctory in the case of illusion. Not even perfunctory: indeed, it would be truer to say that it misses the mark.

In illusion or delusion—that is to say, in the most common form of the setting aside of the real—there is no refusal of perception, strictly so called. The thing perceived is not denied but simply displaced, shifted elsewhere. So far as the ability to see is concerned, the deluded individual sees as clearly as anyone else. This apparently paradoxical truth becomes quite palpable as soon as we think of what happens in the case of the 'blinded' individual, as we see in concrete, daily experience or in novels and drama. For example, the character Alceste in Molière's *Misanthrope* (1666) sees clearly—perfectly and in every way—that Célimène is a *cocotte*. That perception, which he receives every day without turning a hair, is never questioned. And yet Alceste is blind—not because he does not see but because he does not attune his actions to his perception. What he sees is disconnected by him, as it were, from the rest of his life: Célimène's coquetry is perceived and accepted but it is oddly separated from the effects that ought normally to follow at the practical level from its recognition. We may say that the deluded person's perception is, as it were, *split in two*: the *theoretical* aspect (which—from the Greek *theorein*—refers precisely to 'what is seen') artificially frees itself from the *practical* aspect ('what is done'). This is, moreover, why the ultimately 'normal' deluded man is, at heart, much sicker than the neurotic, insofar as he, unlike the neurotic, is resolutely incurable. The blinded individual is incurable, not in his blindness but in his sightedness, as it is impossible to 'make him see again' something he has already seen and still sees. One 'remonstrates' with him in vain, for further *monstration* is impossible with someone who has before his very eyes what you are proposing to show him. In repression and foreclosure, the real may eventually come back, by way of an apparent 'return of the repressed' (if psychoanalysis is to be believed) in dreams and parapraxes. But in illusion this is a vain hope: the real will never return, because it is already there. The

reader will note, in passing, what an anodine and, ultimately, benign case the psychoanalyst's patient represents by comparison with the normal human being.

The most perfect literary example of the rejection
of reality is perhaps offered by Georges Courteline in
his famous play *Boubouroche* (1893).[2] Boubouroche has
installed his mistress, Adèle, in a little flat. Out of the
kindness of his heart, a neighbour of Adèle informs
Boubouroche that he is being betrayed by her on a daily
basis. Adèle is sharing her flat with a young lover who
hides in a cupboard each time Boubouroche visits his
mistress. Mad with rage, Boubouroche bursts in on
Adèle at an unaccustomed time of day and discovers the
lover in the cupboard. Adèle meets Boubouroche's
anger with an annoyed, indignant silence: 'You are so
vulgar,' she tells her protector, 'that you don't even
deserve the very simple explanation I would have given
to anyone else, if he had not been so coarse-mannered.
It is best that you leave.' Boubouroche immediately
admits he is in the wrong and that his suspicions are
unfounded. After being pardoned by Adèle, he has no
other recourse than to turn against the neighbour, the
vile slanderer ('You are an old fool, a simpleton'). This
little play immediately recommends itself to us by an
unusual characteristic. Contrary to the usual course of
events, the dupe is not appeased by some excuse or
explanation. The spectacle of his misfortune is not
veiled by any shadow. The element of deceit is effectively skipped: the dupe has no need of being deceived;
just being a dupe is enough. This is because the illusion

does not lie in what is seen, in what is perceived, which explains why one can, like Boubouroche, be duped, while in fact being duped by *nothing*. And yet Boubouroche, though he enjoys a correct view of events, though he has caught his rival in his hiding place, continues nonetheless to believe in his mistress' innocence. This 'blindness' deserves closer attention.

Let us imagine that, at the wheel of my car, I am, for one reason or another, in a very great hurry to get to my destination and I come to a red light. I can resign myself to the delay it will cause me, stop my vehicle and wait for the light to go green—acceptance of the real. I can also reject a perception that thwarts my plans. In that case, I decide to ignore the prohibition and pass at red. In other words, I take it upon myself not to see a real whose existence I have recognized—the attitude of Oedipus putting out his own eyes. Alternatively, still assuming that I reject the perception, I may rapidly come to the view that this obstacle in my way will cause me more pain than my capacity to adapt to the real can bear. I decide, then, to end it all by committing suicide with a revolver kept in the glove compartment, or I 'repress' the image of the red light into my unconscious. Buried in this way, the red light I went through will never manage to resurface in my consciousness unless a psychoanalyst or a policeman takes a hand. In these last two cases (suicide, repression), I have rejected my perception, ranging this rejection against the need to stop which the perception of the red light would have imposed on me. But, there is yet another means of ignoring this need, which is distinct from all the previous ones in that it does justice to the real, thus attuning itself—at least in appearance—with 'normal' perception: I perceive that the light is red, *but I conclude from this that I am right to pass through it.*

This is exactly what happens to Boubouroche. The reasoning that reassures him could be stated more or less as follows: 'There is a young man in the cupboard—therefore Adèle is innocent and I am not a cuckold.' This is the fundamental structure of illusion: it is the art of seeing true but getting the consequences all wrong. Deluded individuals turn the single event they perceive into two non-coincidental events, with the result that the thing they perceive is put elsewhere, into a place where it *cannot merge with itself.* It is entirely as though the event were magically split in two or, rather, as though two aspects of the same event each came to assume an autonomous existence. In the case of Boubouroche, the fact that Adèle hid a lover and the fact that he is cuckolded become miraculously independent of one another. Descartes would say that Boubouroche's illusion consists in mistaking a 'formal distinction' for a 'real distinction': Boubouroche is incapable of grasping the essential connection which, in the *cogito*, binds the 'I think' to the 'I am'. This is an exemplary connection and, from one of its innumerable applications, Boubouroche would learn that it is impossible to distinguish *really* between 'my wife is deceiving me' and 'I am a cuckold.'

There is another remarkable example of such an illusion, entirely analogous to that of Boubouroche, in

Proust's *Un Amour de Swann* (1913). One day, as he is preparing to send his usual 'monthly payment' to Odette (who had originally been introduced to him as a kept woman, a thing he had forgotten the moment he had fallen in love with her), Swann suddenly wonders whether the act does not amount precisely to 'keeping' a woman; whether the fact of a woman receiving money from a man, as Odette is doing from him, does not indeed coincide with the fact of being what is called a 'kept woman'. This is a fleeting perception of the real, which Swann's love for Odette quickly strikes from his mind:

> He could not study this idea in greater depth, because an attack of that mental laziness which in him was congenital, intermittent and provi-dential, happened at that moment to extinguish all light in his intelligence, as abruptly as, later, when electric lighting had been installed every-where, one could cut off the electricity in a house. His mind groped for a moment in the darkness, he took off his glasses, wiped the lenses, passed his hand over his eyes, and saw the light again only when he found himself in the presence of an entirely different idea, namely that he ought to try to send six or seven thousand francs to Odette next month instead of five, because of the surprise and pleasure it would give her.[3]

Such 'mental lethargy' consists essentially in sepa-rating into two what is actually one, in distinguishing between the woman who is loved and the woman receiving payment; and Proust is quite right to describe this lethargy as 'congenital'. But it should be added that it is neither peculiar to Swann nor to lovers and their passion. It affects the entire human race and represents the main form of illusion to which it is subject: turning a single fact into two divergent facts, a single idea into two distinct ideas—one of them painful, but the other, as Proust rightly puts it, 'wholly different'.

The exemplary blindness of Boubouroche (and Swann) provides us with a clue to the very deep connection that binds illusion to duplication, to the *double*. Like anyone labouring under an illusion, Boubouroche splits the single event into two: he does not suffer from being blind but from *seeing double*. And Adèle does, in fact, say to him at one point: 'You were seeing double,' though, admittedly, in a rather different sense, but the words are, nonetheless, astonishingly premonitory and meaningful. The general technique of illusion is, in fact, to turn one thing into two, as is the way with the illusionist who relies on this same effect of displacement and duplication on the part of the spectator. While he is working on the matter in hand, he directs the onlooker *elsewhere*, to the place where nothing is happening. This is what Adèle is saying to Boubouroche: 'It's true there's a man in the cupboard—but look to one side, here, at how I love you.'

It is the aim of the following chapters to illustrate this connection between illusion and the double, to show that the fundamental structure of illusion is, in fact, the paradoxical structure of the double. I say 'paradoxical', because the notion of double, as we shall see, in itself implies a paradox: namely, that it is both *itself* and *the other*.

In general, the theme of the double is associated primarily with phenomena relating to (schizophrenic or paranoid) split personality and with literature, particularly of the Romantic period, where multiple echoes of it are found. It is as though this theme related essentially to the fringes of psychological normality and, in terms of literature, to a certain Romantic and Modern period. As we shall see, this is not the case at all and the theme of the double is present in an infinitely wider cultural space. That is to say, it is present in the entire space of illusion. It is already present, for example, in the oracular illusion that is part of Greek tragedy and its derivatives (duplication of the event) or in the metaphysical illusion inherent in philosophies of an idealist bent (duplication of the real in general: the 'other world').

Notes

1   William Shakespeare, *Hamlet*, 3.1.78–84. All references to Shakespeare in this volume are from the Oxford Standard Authors edition of *Shakespeare: Complete Works* (W. J. Craig ed.) (Oxford: Oxford University Press, 1905).

2   See Georges Courteline, *Boubouroche* in *The Plays of Courteline*, VOL. 1 (Albert Bermel ed., Jacques Barzun and Albert Bermel trans) (New York: Theatre Arts Books, 1961), pp. 60–86.

3   Marcel Proust, *In Search of Lost Time*, Part 1, *The Way by Swann's* (Lydia Davis trans.) (London: Penguin, 2003), p. 271.

CHAPTER ONE

THE ORACULAR ILLUSION:
THE EVENT AND ITS DOUBLE

It is both a general and a paradoxical characteristic of oracles that their predictions come to pass and yet occasion surprise as they do so. The oracle obligingly announces the event in advance, with the result that the person destined to undergo it has time to prepare for it and, potentially, to attempt to stave it off. Now, the event occurs as predicted (or as announced by a dream or some other premonitory phenomenon), but that occurrence curiously disappoints expectations at the very point when they ought to be regarded as fulfilled. A is announced, A happens—and yet, we can't make sense of it. Or, at least, not exactly. Between the event announced and the event that occurs, there is a kind of subtle difference that is enough to disturb the person who was, nonetheless, expecting precisely what he is now seeing. He finds what he is expecting but loses his bearings. And yet, nothing has taken place except the predicted event. But, inexplicably, that event is *other*.

One of Aesop's fables, 'The Son and the Painted Lion'—a fable that exists in many other versions, both ancient and modern—illustrates this feature which generally applies to the fulfilment of oracles:

> There was a timid old man who was afraid of his only son's passion for hunting, for the son was full of courage. In a dream he saw that his son would be killed by a lion. Dreading that this dream would come true, the father built a dwelling for his son of great magnificence, set in a high place where he could keep his eye on him. In order to distract and please him, he had commissioned for his chamber paintings of every kind of animal, and among these was a lion. But looking at all these did not distract the young man from his boredom.
>
> One day he approached the painting and cursed the lion in it:
>
> 'You damned beast, it's because of you and my father's lying dream that I'm cooped up here in this prison for women. What can I do to you?'
>
> And, as he said this, he struck his fist against the wall to blind the lion. But a splinter got lodged under his fingernail and he could not get it out. This became greatly inflamed, brought on a fever and swelled up to an

enormous size. The fever raged so fiercely that the young man died of it.

The lion, even though it was only a painted one, had indeed killed the young man, just as his father had foreseen.[1]

Leaving aside the moral supplied by Aesop—who simply notes that 'we should bravely face the fate which awaits us, rather than try to outwit or trick Fate, for what is destined cannot be evaded'—what is this about? Quite clearly at issue here is *destiny* and, in the event, the *tricks* it plays. That is to say, the real—the sum of the events that are called into existence—is presented as inevitable (as destiny), as fated to occur in spite of each and every effort made to prevent it (even by way of a 'trick'). If one happens to be warned in advance of this necessity that is inherent in every occurrence—and hence, theoretically, in a position to stave it off—destiny will respond with a ruse that will thwart the effort to parry it and will even, at times, delight (this is its *irony*) in turning the intended obstacle into the means by which it comes to pass, with the result that, in cases of this kind, the person who strives to prevent the feared event becomes the engineer of his own downfall, and destiny—out of elegance or indolence—entrusts its victims with doing the work in its stead. This, as has always rightly been said, is the most manifest meaning of these kinds of fable. But, beyond this primary meaning, there is perhaps another that is richer and more general. Evidence of this is to be found in the fact that this fable—and every similar story—continues to

3

interest us, continues to point up for the listener some deep truth that is independent of any consideration of destiny and its tricks. Those who know there has never been anything resembling destiny and inevitability— among them La Fontaine who, taking up Aesop's fable, derives from it an opposing moral, equating the effects of destiny with 'effects of chance'[2]—and who recognize every fable elaborating on these themes as a retro- spective reconstruction aimed at putting the stamp of necessity on a chance series of events, nonetheless recognize the echo of a certain truth in these depictions of destiny. Something, it seems, is being said in these stories.

That something is clearly linked, in the first instance, to the sense of having been *tricked*. We have been, we say, a mere plaything in the hands of destiny. Once the illusion of destiny has passed, the sense of having been a plaything remains—the sense of having been toyed with. Exactly in the same way as, in fencing or some other activity, one may be surprised by a feint. We defend ourselves on the left and, yet, we are attacked on the right. And, in protecting ourselves, it is the very spot which is vulnerable that we leave undefended, so that the evasive action merges with the fatal strike. Even more than this, the evasive move and the fatal strike are merely one and the same action, like Heraclitus' mysterious path, which goes up and down at the same time.[3] The oracle came to pass only with the aid of this misguided precaution, and the very act of avoiding destiny coincides with destiny's fulfilment. To such a degree, indeed, that the prophecy announces nothing but the unfortunate evasive action. This ironic or, more precisely, elliptical structure of the fulfilment of oracles occurs very frequently and may even be said to constitute one of the preferred themes of oracular literature.

We may note, to begin with, that this failure of 'defence' is merely a rather banal aspect of human finitude. To protect oneself effectively, to be entirely safe, we would have to be able to think of everything at once. Now, we know that human beings, though they possess the privilege of thought, have not received the gift of intellectual ubiquity: they think something at a given time and nothing else at that particular moment. This is why they may always be easy prey, for, while they are on their guard in one area, there will always be a thousand others in which they can be attacked. This fragility, which is the subject of Franz Kafka's 'The Burrow' (1923–24), is what lends profundity to the Nzakara saying from the Central African Republic, as reported by Anne Retel-Laurentin: 'Who knows what may come from the *other* end of the village?'[4]

Yet, the deception attaching to the human being's poor defence against destiny is not merely the mark of a finitude. It also points to a deception of a quite other order, which has to do not, in this case, with—absent, non-existent—destiny but with the very consciousness of the person who feels he has been deceived. It is obvious there is no destiny; it is also obvious that, in the absence of any destiny, there are such things as cunning, illusion and deception. Since these cannot be ascribed to an unanswerable—because non-existent—destiny, we have to find an origin for them in something more answerable and tangible. If it is the case that what occurred surprised us even as it fulfilled our expectation, then the expectation is to blame, not the occurrence. The source of the deception is to be sought not in the event but in the expectation. The analysis of thwarted expectation reveals that, parallel to the perception of what occurred, a spontaneous idea is created that the event, in coming to pass, eliminated another version of the event—the actual version that we were expecting. This is a very strong impression, to use David Hume's terms while slightly modifying his meaning, for it is remarkable that the impression of having foreseen something other than what really occurred—an impression that might have some semblance of foundation in the case of the oracle in the aforementioned Aesop's fable (the king's son could have been killed by a flesh-and-blood lion)—persists even in cases where it can be established that no version of the event was really foreseen or represented—nor indeed foreseeable or representable —before it actually took place.

Three other examples will suffice to illustrate this strange capacity the oracle possesses to surprise us, while not actually disappointing any genuine expectation: the legend of Oedipus, as depicted in Sophocles' *Oedipus Rex;* the story of Segismundo in Pedro Calderón de la Barca's *Life is a Dream* (1635); and an Arabic tale told by Jacques Deval in his play *Tonight in Samarkand* (1950).

THE LEGEND OF OEDIPUS: an oracle predicted to the sovereigns of Thebes, Laius and Jocasta, that their son Oedipus would kill his father and marry his mother. Abandoned at birth on a mountainside, Oedipus is taken in by the sovereigns of Corinth, Polybus and Merope, who, in the absence of any heir, adopt him and raise him as their son. Learning of the prediction hanging over his head, Oedipus suddenly leaves Corinth and his supposed parents, attempting to escape his destiny. On the way, he meets his real father and kills him, solves the riddle of the Sphinx and enters Thebes in triumph to marry his mother, the widow of the dead king.

THE STORY OF SEGISMUNDO: Basil, king of Poland, has drawn up his son Segismundo's horoscope at his birth and found that the stars destine his son to become the cruellest monarch who ever lived—'a monster in human form'—whose first concern would be to turn his savage strength on his father, the king, and trample him underfoot. Frightened by these sinister auguries, he has Segismundo locked up in a lonely tower that affords him no possibility of contact with others, except his tutor, Clotaldo. When Segismundo comes of age, his father frees him for a day and presents him at court, so as to confirm the truth of the horoscope, at which point, infuriated by twenty years of captivity, Segismundo behaves in keeping with the prediction. After being taken back to his tower, then freed by a popular uprising, Segismundo—who no longer knows whether he is awake or dreaming—fulfils the prediction of the horoscope: he becomes leader of the uprising and defeats his father, who has no choice than to throw himself at his feet and appeal to his improbable mercy. But the horoscope had predicted things only up to this point and, in keeping with the usual oracular structure, the drama ends in a way that is both unexpected and consonant with the prediction, since the play's conclusion betrays expectations while squaring precisely with the oracle: mollified by his doubt as to what is real, Segismundo helps his father to his feet and pays him the respect due to his royal blood.

THE ARABIC TALE: Once upon a time in Baghdad, there was a caliph and his vizier. One day, the vizier came before the caliph, pale and trembling. 'Pardon my great dread, O Light of the Faithful,' he said, 'but outside the palace, a woman bumped into me in the crowd. I turned round and that woman, with a pale complexion and dark hair, a red scarf about her neck, was Death. Seeing me, she beckoned . . . Since Death is looking for me here, Lord, let me flee and hide, far from this place, in Samarkand. If I hurry I can be there before nightfall.' So saying, he galloped off on his horse and vanished in a cloud of dust in the direction of Samarkand. The caliph then left his palace and he too met Death. 'Why did you frighten my vizier who is young and well?' asked the caliph. And Death replied, 'I did not mean to frighten him, but seeing him in Baghdad surprised me, since I was expecting him this evening in Samarkand.'

There is an obvious structural similarity between the three stories. In all three, the prediction is fulfilled by the very act that strives to avert its fulfilment. Oedipus, Basil and the vizier meet their destiny through attempting to avoid it. It is by leaving Corinth that Oedipus sets out towards a meeting with his real parents; it is by locking his son away that Basil makes him the monster foretold in the horoscope; and it is by rushing to Samarkand that the vizier goes to the death he is trying to escape. But this structure is common to most stories enacting the fulfilment of oracles. The focus here, however, is on another—stranger, more profound—feature: on the fact that the three heroes of this same misadventure would be equally incapable, if asked, of giving a precise account of the nature of their deception. All three have been deceived but none of them could say what the expected event was that the real event has overwritten unexpectedly or 'obliquely', to use the adjective that qualifies the Delphic oracle, Apollo Loxias. The dreaded event took place but it occurred *thwarting the expectation of the same event* which was, admittedly, supposed to take place but in another way. However, it is impossible to say what this 'other' way is.

If one is in any doubt on this point, one has only to consult the parties concerned and ask them kindly to clarify what the version of the dreaded event in their minds was before the real event replaced it. If questioned, the Vizir will reply that he was indeed expecting to die that evening but not in that way or at that place (Samarkand): he feared death in *another* way and at *another* place. 'What other way? What other place? I do not know, but neither this evening nor at Samarkand.'

Basil, the king of Poland, will reply that he knew very well his son would use violence and bring him to the ground: however, not in the completely unexpected way assumed by the event. In what other way, then? Basil could expect the event to happen only in that place where he had countered it and hoped to have made its execution impossible: it will not take much to make him admit that, having rendered the event impossible in 'normal' conditions, he was not afraid of any precise fulfilment of the horoscope's prediction and his surprise at the way it actually found confirmation did not result from the fact that that confirmation negated some other possibility of its realization. The real version of the facts in the mind of the king does not, then, contradict any other version or, at least, seems only to contradict a ghostly version that was never actually conceptualized.

On first examination, the case of Oedipus seems more complex. Oedipus kills his father and marries his mother without knowing their respective identities. Hence, the fulfilment of the oracle contradicts a version of the event which, in this case, has a precise content: the murder of Polybus and marriage with Merope, the rulers of Corinth whom Oedipus believes to be his parents. However, this is an abstract view of the matter that cannot be given concrete form in a real narrative: since he has been warned of the threat hanging over his fate, Oedipus, leaving Corinth in haste, has decided to lay hands neither on Polybus nor on Merope. Given all that, the question remains: How could Oedipus go about killing his father and marrying his mother, except by killing a man accidentally and marrying a woman by chance who turn out to be his father and mother respectively, while not being Polybus or Merope? And yet, it will be said, the way Oedipus fulfils the prophecy is a trick of destiny. That is true, but what other trick might be envisaged? No precise answer to this question (itself oblique) is to be expected—except the answer that consists in stubbornly reasserting that the event was expected elsewhere and in another way, without it ever being possible to specify the nature of that 'elsewhere' or that 'other way'.

One might, admittedly, envisage the extreme hypothesis of Polybus and Merope being his real parents and Oedipus killing the one and marrying the other by accident or mistake. We might, for example, imagine an attack of maniacal anger, a sleepwalking incident or some sort of disguise that would prevent Oedipus from recognizing the man he killed as Polybus or the woman he married as Merope. This theme of disguise is, moreover, present at a deep (but symbolic) level in the real destiny of Oedipus, since his real parents are, so to speak, disguised beneath alien features, since they borrow 'living masks' from the faces of Polybus and Merope behind which to conceal their own persons. But, if we examine the hypothetical case in which Polybus and Merope were Oedipus' actual parents, they would not appear disguised as other living persons. They would simply be made up in such a way or would intervene in such circumstances that Oedipus would not recognize them—rather like the legend of St Julian the Hospitaller, who also tries to escape a prediction and ends up fulfilling it by killing his parents by mistake. This hypothesis in Oedipus' case is, in any event, barely credible, since Oedipus has left Corinth and his parents never to return: Where then could he meet his disguised parents? We would have to accept the idea here that Polybus and Merope would set off in search of their fleeing son, abandoning their royal responsibilities. And this new hypothesis, which is even more incredible, is not, in fact, sufficient to make murder of the one and marriage with the other possible, since Oedipus would always run from his parents, wherever they eventually found him. The prophecy could not be fulfilled through a fit of anger or somnambulism, since Oedipus would always be long gone. The only remaining possibility, then, is that of a mistake, as a result of perfect disguise. One evening, leaving a Theban tavern where he has drunk too much wine, Oedipus meets Polybus, who is made up to be unrecognizable and searching incognito for his son. Oedipus gets into a quarrel with him and kills him. Some days later, again in his cups, Oedipus meets a poor woman in the street, falls in love with her and takes her as his wife: this is Merope, so well disguised that, after several months of conjugal life, he still doesn't recognize his new wife as his mother. This version of events is just about imaginable; one might, indeed, imagine many other possible ways in which the oracle might be fulfilled. But the fact that such itineraries are possible and imaginable in no way explains the surprise that accompanies the discovery of the actual slant taken by the fulfilment of the oracle—a surprise linked to the vague sense that the real event has taken the place of an event that was *more expected* and *more plausible*.

Yet, all the possible versions seem, ultimately, much more improbable than the actual story which, nonetheless, came as a surprise. If Polybus and Merope are indeed Oedipus' parents, the fulfilment of the oracle will have to go down much more complicated, unexpected avenues than the real version. The hypothesis of a substitute paternity—that is, that Polybus and Merope are not Oedipus' real parents—is, all in all, the *simplest* way from the oracle to its fulfilment. If, then, the fulfilment of the oracle comes as a surprise, it is not because its form is unexpected in comparison to another that would be less so. How could an event A be seen as highly improbable in comparison to an event B if it turns out that this event B is itself, in the best of scenarios, much more improbable yet? Supposing that this other version of Oedipus' destiny, apparently more consonant with the oracle, came to pass, would it not, in its turn, contrast starkly with a thousand other versions that would then be seen—with greater justification—as much more probable? The fulfilment of Oedipus' fate—as sealed by the oracle—does not, then, eliminate any possibility that is equally or more probable than the one chosen in the end by reality—all that is imaginable here being more complicated and more improbable than what will turn out to be the real event. Though the wording of the oracle may be described as 'oblique', the route by which Oedipus fulfils his destiny is, by contrast, the straightest of straight paths: he has not taken any roundabout road, and this is perhaps precisely what is known as a 'trick' of destiny—going straight to the goal, not lingering on the way, moving directly towards oneself.

Despite this analysis, an impression remains, nonetheless, that we have been trapped by a cunning, omnipotent fate that thwarts all the means deployed to circumvent it. But, this fate now takes on a more exact meaning, precisely insofar as we have now recognized its vagueness: the fateful event brings us up short by overwriting another we have never thought about at all, never had any idea of. The surprise here has itself an unexpected character: it consists, in fact, in rejecting the real event in the name of an event we would never imagine, of a reality that never has been—and never will be—conceived. The event has taken the place of an 'other' event but that other event is itself nothing. What comes into focus here is the sensation of being tricked that is experienced by someone who is expecting an event but is amazed to see that event occur. There is, indeed, deception somewhere, but the deception actually lies in the illusion of being deceived, in the belief that there is 'something' that can, in fact, be said to have been replaced by the coming-to-pass of the event. Hence, it is the sense of being deceived that is deceptive here. In happening, the event has merely happened. It has not taken the place of another event.

Of course, one cannot, for all this, deny the ambiguity inherent in prophetic speech, nor the double meanings repeatedly found in oracles and tragedy. It is simply a question of seeing that this ambiguity does not consist in the splitting of what is said into two possible meanings but, rather, in the way two meanings coincide—meanings which we only retrospectively see are two in appearance but one in reality. Sophocles' *Oedipus Rex* is rich in examples of this ambiguity, the most elementary and profoundest of them being the speech in which Oedipus implies that he is both the person he is and that other whom he is seeking:

> 'The king proudly declares: By going right back, in my turn, to the beginning [of the events that have remained unknown] I am the one who will bring them to light [εγω φανω].' The scholiast does not fail to point out that something lies hidden in the *ego phano*, something that Oedipus did not mean but that the spectator understands, 'since everything will be discovered in Oedipus himself [επει το παν εν αυιω φανησεται].' *Ego phano* means 'It is I who will bring the criminal to light' but also 'I shall discover myself to be the criminal.'[5]

It is clear that, in saying 'εγω φανω' (*ego phano*)—'I shall show' and 'I shall appear'—Oedipus is saying two things at once; but it is no less clear that these two things are one and the same. What counts here is that you hear only a single truth, whereas you believe you are hearing

15

two. Sophocles' play, a tragedy of coincidence and not of ambiguity, unfolds towards an implacable return to the unique, which eliminates, scene by scene, the illusion of a possible duplication—with the result that Sophoclean tragedy is not at all associated with double meaning but, rather, with the progressive elimination of it. Oedipus' misfortune is that he is only himself and not two people. It is to mistake his misfortune—and, in a sense, to fall into the very trap Oedipus falls into in Sophocles' play—to say, as J.-P. Vernant does: 'What then is Oedipus? Like his own discourse, like the pronouncement of the oracle, Oedipus is double, enigmatic.'[6] For the mystery of Oedipus is, precisely, that he is *single* and not double, just as the mystery of the Sphinx, solved by Oedipus in a kind of preview of his destiny, lies in its referring to oneself and not to another.

It is, ultimately, the same with the fulfilment of any oracle. The awaited event ultimately coincides with itself. Hence the surprise: one was expecting something different, though related; expecting the same thing but not exactly this way. All the 'tricks' of destiny come down in the last analysis to this strict coincidence of what was foreseen with what actually happened. The trick delivers the event itself here and now, whereas we were expecting it to be a little different and to occur some little way off and not immediately. This is the paradoxical nature of the surprise we feel in response to the fulfilment of oracles: we are astonished, though the grounds for astonishment have precisely been removed, the event having matched its foretelling

16

exactly. The event we were expecting to happen did happen. However, we then see that it was not *this* event we were expecting but the identical event in a different form. We thought we were expecting the same but, in reality, we were expecting the other.

It is time now to recognize in this 'other event' ('expected', perhaps, but never conceived or imagined), which the real event overwrote with its own occurrence, the fundamental structure of the *double*. There is, in fact, nothing to distinguish this other event from the real event, except for the confused conception that it is both the same and another—which is the exact definition of the double. In this way, we find a very profound relationship between oracular thought and the fantasy of duplication, which explains the enigmatic surprise attached to the spectacle of the fulfilled oracle. The fulfilment of the oracle ultimately surprises insofar as it removes the possibility of any duplication. By happening, the predicted event renders null and void the prediction of a possible double. In coming to existence, it eliminates its double; and it is the disappearance of this pale ghost of the real that surprises consciousness for a moment when the event occurs. Hence, the formula that normally greets the discovery of that which was expected—'It was just that'—implies both a recognition and a disowning. A recognition of the event foretold; a disowning because the event did not occur in another way. The recognition and the disowning are thus inseparable and ultimately mean the same thing: a gazing upon the structure of the *unique*. The unique fulfils expectation by coming to pass but disappoints that expectation by striking out any other mode of its realization. And this is, in fact, the fate of any event in the world.

In a passage in his study, 'The Memory of the Present and False Recognition' (1908), Henri Bergson confirms this connection between the oracular structure (prediction, a sense of the inevitable) and the theme of the double. Analyzing the illusion that afflicts certain subjects whose perceptions are doubled and who have the impression of experiencing things twice, so to speak—once in the present and once in the mode of memory—Bergson refers, sure enough, to the theme of destiny:

> What is said and done, what one says and does oneself seem 'inevitable'. One is a spectator to one's own impulses, thoughts and actions. Things happen *as though* one were split, without one actually being split. One of the subjects writes: 'This sense of splitting [*dédoublement*] exists only in terms of sensation; the two persons are one and the same from the material point of view.' By this he doubtless means that he experiences a sense of duality, but accompanied by the awareness that only a single person is involved. Moreover, as we were saying at the beginning, the subject often finds himself in the peculiar state of mind of a person who believes he knows what is going to happen while feeling incapable of predicting it.[7]

It is noticeable that the theme of prediction appears here, linked, as ever, to the theme of surprise (one predicts something without, however, expecting its concrete realization and, hence, that realization will always be a source of amazement).

However, any duplication presupposes an original and a copy, and the question will be which of the two—the real event or the 'other event'—is the model and which its double. We then discover that the 'other event' isn't really the double of the real event. In fact, the opposite is true: it is the real event that seems itself to be the double of the 'other event'. It is, as a result, the real event that is, ultimately, the 'other': the other is *this* real, or the double of another real that may be said to be the real itself but which always eludes us and of which we shall never be able to say or know anything. The unique, the real and the event thus possess this extraordinary quality of being, so to speak, the *other of nothing*, of appearing to be the double of an *other* reality that constantly vanishes on the threshold of realization, at the moment of any coming-to-be-real. The entirety of the events that occur—that is to say, reality in its entirety—represents merely a kind of 'bad' real, belonging to the order of the double, the copy, the image: it is the *other* which this real has struck out that is the absolute real, the true original, for which the real event is merely a deceptive, perverse stand-in. The true real is elsewhere: it may be said to reside, to take our three examples, in a parricide and an incest that are different from those awaiting Oedipus, in an aggressiveness on the part of

Segismundo unrelated to the actual circumstances of his childhood, in a death somewhere other than in Samarkand. As for the events that really happened, they are like apings of that real: and the entirety of real events thus appears like an enormous caricature of reality. It is in this sense that life is merely a dream, an untrue fable or, alternatively, as Macbeth has it, a tale told by an idiot. The sense of being duped by reality—which expresses the most general truth of oracular stories—of being deceived constantly by the false real that substitutes itself at the last moment for the true real which we have never seen and will never happen, may be rendered by the popular expression that certain realities, certain acts are, precisely, 'not on'. And this does not apply only to certain 'realizations' or certain acts: everything, by occurring, becomes 'not on' in this way. And this is a truth that had already been expressed by the philosophers of Megara, and deepened by Bergson in the first three chapters of *La Pensée et le mouvant* (1934):[8] *it is the fate of all reality to place itself outside the range of the possible*. The argument will be, then, that the real event is, in some way or another, rigged and that it is playing fast and loose with the real. And to use a naive terminology consonant with what are themselves naive sentiments, it will be possible to say that the event that happened is not 'the right one'. The right event, the event that would alone be entitled to pronounce itself truly real, is actually the one that did not take place, the one that was stifled at birth by its 'rigged' double. The real event, in the ordinary sense of the term, is thus always 'other than the right one'.

It will be evident here that all reality, even if it has not been announced by an oracle or foreseen in some premonition or the like, is oracular in structure in the sense defined above. It is, in fact, the fate of everything that exists to deny, by its very existence, any form of different reality. Now, it is the peculiarity of oracles that they suggest—without ever exactly specifying—something other than the thing they announce, other than the thing that does actually occur. But this thwarted suggestion may manifest itself at any point, for every event implies the negation of its double. This is why every occasion is oracular (realizing the *other* of its double) and every existence a crime (for killing off its double). This is the fate invisibly attaching to the real, which makes Segismundo, locked up in his tower, say that man's greatest crime is to have been born at all, or E. M. Cioran that we lost everything when we were born— hence the title *The Trouble with Being Born*.[9] In this regard, every event is both a murder and a marvel. If, for example, in a ticket system for queuing, I take number 138, then I eliminate, at a stroke, 998 other possibilities. This is a 'trouble' and it is also a marvel, provided we forget that, though an event can, at a pinch, occur in any way whatsoever, it must necessarily occur in *some* way. I cannot both be Cioran and someone other than Cioran, even if it seems to me confusedly that it is only by some arbitrary—and, ultimately, rather disappointing— decree that I am indeed Cioran and not someone else.

We may observe in this connection that the occurrence of an event that is not predicted by an oracle but simply foreseen by common sense, observing the circumstances and a set of premonitory signs, is always surprising, in the same way as oracles may surprise us. That is to say, the surprise in both cases consists in the fact that A is indeed A and not B. It is the trick of fate, as it is of rational foresight, to spirit away the double from the single, unique event. There is a radio announcement, one morning, that the condition of the president could not be worse. Yet, when his death is announced in the evening, it surprises us (so it *was* that way, then; A was *indeed* A). And it is because of this ever-surprising nature of events that the notion of destiny, suggested by oracles, assumes a real, universal meaning. For, when all is said and done, destiny *is* at issue in oracular legends but in a much more profound sense than is immediately apparent. There is indeed something that exists which is called destiny; however, it refers not to the inevitable character of what happens but to its unpredictable nature. There is, in fact, a destiny wholly independent of any necessity and predictability and, hence, independent of any oracular phenomenon, though, in a sense, the oracle speaks of it in its way, and it is the destiny both of human beings and of every existing thing. The meaning of this destiny, which is apparently paradoxical, since it is alien to the notion of necessity that seems, in fact, to provide the main—or only—basis for it, is linked to an exactly opposite notion: to the certainty of unpredictability. But it is just this certainty that the oracular literature speaks of in veiled terms. One can always be sure of being surprised; one can always firmly expect never to be able to expect.

All in all, the profundity and truth of oracular speech lie less in predicting the future than in expressing the suffocating necessity of the present, the ineluctable character of what is happening *now*. Prediction has a predominantly symbolic value: it is a simple projection into time of what awaits the human being at every moment of his present life. At every moment, this is what faces him and nothing else. Whether the circumstances are happy or sad, whether he triumphs or is dying, he is up against it. There is no way out—no double. This is what the oracle—rightly—announced in advance. 'One does not escape fate' means, quite simply, that one does not escape the real—that which is and cannot but be. This is more or less what Lady Macbeth says to her husband, that other illustrious victim of oracular literature: 'What's done is done.'[10] What exists is forever univocal: doubles dissipate on the threshold of the real, by enchantment or by malediction, depending on whether the event is favourable or unfavourable. All that remains is the event coinciding with itself, as at the end of *Macbeth* when the prediction is fulfilled and 'Birnam wood / Do come to Dunsinane.'[11] A comes to merge with A, as Oedipus merges with himself at the end of *Oedipus Rex*.

Before hurling himself into a last battle against his own destiny—that is, against himself—Macbeth pronounces the famous words: 'Life . . . is a tale / Told by an idiot, full of sound and fury, / Signifying nothing.'[12] The idea of chaos and meaninglessness thus wins out in the moment of contact with the real. The fact is that, until the last moment, Macbeth, like every human being (in the hour of death, for example), expects that A will differ ever so slightly from A, that the event will not be exactly what it is. The coincidence of the real with itself, which is, from a certain standpoint, simplicity itself and the most limpid version of the real, appears the greatest absurdity in the eyes of the deluded or, in other words, of those who, to the end, were banking on the grace of a double. A real that is merely the real and nothing else is meaningless, absurd—idiotic, as Macbeth puts it. And Macbeth is right—on this point, at least: reality is indeed idiotic, since, before it meant stupid, the word 'idiotic' meant simple, particular, unique of its kind. Such is reality and all the events that make it up: simple, particular, unique—*idiotès*—'idiotic'.

This idiocy of reality is a fact that has always been recognized by metaphysicians, who repeat that the 'meaning' of the real is not to be found here, but elsewhere. The metaphysical dialectic is fundamentally a dialectic of here and elsewhere, of a 'here' that is doubted or rejected and an 'elsewhere' from which salvation is expected to come. Decidedly, A cannot be reduced to A: *here* must have light cast on it by an *elsewhere*. 'Time and time again, Asia has sensed that Man's key problem is to grasp "something else",' writes André Malraux, for example,[13] echoing Richard Wagner's romantic utterance in the *Wesendonk-Lieder*: 'Our world is not here.'[14] It is no longer a double of the event that is required, then, but a double of reality in general, 'another world', called upon to account for *this* world, which would, considered solely on its own terms, remain forever 'idiotic'.

The oracular illusion—the doubling of the event—thus finds a wider field of expression in the doubling of the real in general—in the metaphysical illusion.

Notes

1   Aesop, 'Fable 295' in *The Complete Fables* (Olivia and Robert Temple trans) (London: Penguin, 1998), p. 218.

2   The phrase 'effets du hasard' occurs in Jean de la Fontaine's fable 'L'horoscope' (The Horoscope), (BK 8, Fable 16). English translations vary in their rendering of the phrase.

3   'The path up and down is one and the same.' Heraclitus, 'Fragment 60' in *Fragments* (James Hillman ed., Brooks Haxton trans.) (London: Penguin, 2003).

4   J.-P. Vernant, L. Vandermeersch, J. Gemet, J. Bottéro, R. Crahay, L. Brisson, J. Carlier, D. Grodzynski and A. Retel-Laurentin, *Divination et rationalité* (Paris: Seuil, 1974), p. 3.

5   J.-P. Vernant, Pierre Vidal-Naquet, *Myth and Tragedy in Ancient Greece* (Janet Lloyd trans.) (New York: Zone Books, 1990), p. 118.

6   Ibid., pp. 117–18.

7   Henri Bergson, 'L'énergie spirituelle: essais et conférences' in *Oeuvres* (André Robinet ed.) (Paris: Presses universitaires de France, 1959), p. 921. Available in English as *Mind-Energy: Lectures and Essays* (H. Wildon Carr trans.) (New York: Henry Holt, 1920).

8   Henri Bergson, *La pensée et le mouvant: Essais et conférences* (Thought and Motion: Essays and Lectures) (Paris: F. Alcan, 1934).

9 E. M. Cioran, *The Trouble with Being Born* (Richard Howard trans.) (New York: Seaver Books, 1976).

10 William Shakespeare, *Macbeth*, 3.2.12.

11 Ibid., 5.5.44–5.

12 Ibid., 5.6.24–8.

13 André Malraux, *Lazare* (Paris: Gallimard, 1974), p. 131. Available in English as *Lazarus* (Terence Kilmartin trans.) (New York: Grove Press, 1978).

14 Richard Wagner, 'Im Treibhaus: Studie zu Tristan und Isolde' in *Fünf Gedichte von Mathilde Wesendonk für eine Frauenstimme und Klavier*, (Leipzig: C. F. Peters Musikverlag, 1858). [In this song cycle known widely as *Wesendonck-Lieder*, the poet actually writes 'Unsre Heimat ist nicht hier' (Our home is not here), but Rosset is quoting from a French translation which renders the line as: 'Notre monde n'est point ici.'—Trans.]

CHAPTER TWO

THE METAPHYSICAL ILLUSION: THE WORLD AND ITS DOUBLE

The duplication of the real, which constitutes the oracular structure of every event, also, when seen from another point of view, constitutes the fundamental structure of metaphysical discourse from Plato to our day. Consonant with this metaphysical structure, the immediately real is accepted and understood only insofar as it may be considered the expression of another real, which alone confers its meaning and reality upon it. *This* world, which has no meaning in and of itself, receives its meaning and its being from another world that doubles it—or, rather, a world of which this world is merely a deceptive doubling. And it is a peculiarity of the 'metaphysical' image that it allows us to sense, beneath the senseless—or falsely meaningful—appearances, the signification and reality that provide its infrastructure and explain precisely the appearance of this world, which is simply 'the at once primordial and trivial manifestation of an amazing mystery.'[1]

This structure of reiteration, in which the other occupies the place of the real and *this* world the place of the double, is none other, once again, than the structure of the oracle: the real that presents itself to us immediately is a doubling, just as the event that really takes place is a sham. It doubles the 'real' in the same way as the fulfilment of the oracle 'doubled' the expected event. Perhaps this impression of having been doubled is not simply the structure of metaphysics but the philosophical illusion par excellence. It will be noted that it is present within philosophies that claim to reject all metaphysics: for example, in the work of Karl Marx, who strives to identify the 'real' law in the apparent real, the law which explains both its meaning and its development, in a move that is doubly oracular (superadded to the duplication of the visible and the invisible, which claims to make the distinction between a 'falsehood' and a 'truth', is prediction, the proclamation of the future). Quite obviously, however, it is in the work of Plato that this structural affinity between oracular philosophy and philosophy *tout court* appears most clearly. The myth of the cave, the myth of Er of Pamphylia and the theory of reminiscence are the most precise expressions of this theme of the duplication of the unique, which makes Platonism in general a philosophy that is oracular in essence.

It might be objected here, drawing on certain passages in Plato,[2] that Platonism is not a philosophy of the double but a 'philosophy of the singular' based precisely on the impossibility of the double.[3] Admittedly, it is, in Plato's view, one of the characteristics of any object that it is inimitable, that there can only ever be one of it. Socrates shows, for example, in the *Cratylus* that the perfect representation of Cratylus would produce not a double (Cratylus twice) but an absurdity; for it is part of Cratylus' essence to be one, not two. That essence, which defines singularity, is by definition imitable, but not duplicable, for it can give rise only to images, which will never, as it happens, have the character of the double. The question is, however, whether the impossibility of duplication or the necessity of the singular lead, in Plato, to a philosophy of the unique. We must here distinguish between two levels of duplication: the sensible level and the metaphysical level. We are, in fact, up against two impossibilities of duplication: on the one hand, the impossibility that the sensible object could duplicate itself in another sensible object that would, at the same time, be itself (the *Cratylus* argument); on the other, the impossiblity that the sensible object could itself appear as the double of a real, supersensible model (the argument stated at the beginning of the *Parmenides*). In the first case, we are speaking of non-repetition at the level of sensible objects; the essence of the sensible object is never to be able to repeat itself—that is, never to be able to reconstitute this same sensible object elsewhere or at another time. This impossibility of repeating itself indeed encapsulates the essence of the sensible and, at the same time, underscores its finitude. It is, precisely, the mark of what is constitutionally unsatisfying about the sensible, when abandoned to itself, that it is never able to 're-present' things, to such a degree that Søren Kierkegaard, in 'Repetition'[4] makes this inability to repeat the main source of the distance he feels from the things of this world (a distance of Platonic inspiration): he cannot, as Alfred de Vigny puts it in 'La maison du berger', 'love what we shall never see twice'.[5] In the second case, from the impossibility of the sensible object (that is, of all the things of this world) repeating a supersensible model (that is, the 'idea' or the absolute 'real'), we deduce the idea of the disappointing character of the real by comparison with that other 'real' it is incapable of duplicating. In both cases, the non-duplicable character of reality leads to a depreciation of the sensible object, which is criticized, precisely, for not being able to be the double—either of itself as a sensible thing or of the other as a primordial reality. All of which means that the impossiblity of the double paradoxically demonstrates that this world *is* merely a double or, more precisely, a bad double, a falsified duplication, incapable of 're-presenting' either the other or itself—in short, it is an apparent reality, entirely woven from a cloth of 'lesser being', which stands in the relation of a by-product to 'being'. The fact that Plato regards duplication as impossible does not at all imply, then, that Platonism is not a philosophy of the double but, rather, the opposite.

The truth of Platonism remains, therefore, firmly attached to the myth of the cave: *this* real is the 'wrong side' of the real world; it is its shadow or its double. And events in the world are merely replicas of real events: they are second moments of a truth whose first moment is elsewhere, in the other world. This, as we know, is the sense of the theory of reminiscence, which teaches that there can never be any genuinely primary experience in this world. Nothing is ever discovered: everything is regained and comes back into memory through being reunited with the original idea. The little slave in the *Menon* makes not a discovery but a rediscovery. The will itself can only re-will what necessity has already commanded from the other world, as the myth of Er of Pamphylia teaches. And, with this way gods have of shipping responsibility for their own decrees onto humans, we come back to the irony of oracular prediction, which consists in entrusting the fulfilment of that prediction to its victims themselves, as in the Aesop fable quoted earlier.

Like any oracular phenomenon, metaphysical thought is based on a quasi-instinctive rejection of the *immediate*, which is suspected of being, so to speak, the other of itself or the doubling of another reality. We may say that it is the very notion of immediacy that appears rigged: the immediate is distrusted precisely because its very immediacy is doubted. This immediate, which is here present, presents itself as primary, but is it not, rather, secondary? Such, perhaps, is the origin of the ancestral mistrust of the 'primary' that finds a meaningful echo in Talleyrand's remark that one should distrust the first impulse since it is generally right. An analysis of this profound remark reveals that we distrust our first impulse, we do not regard it as 'right' precisely because we refuse to take it as 'first': isn't it already a 'secondary elaboration'? Have I not given my intelligence the time to be overtaken by some deceitful interpretation emanating from my desire and, hence, by an image of reality as I would prefer it to be, not reality itself? It is probably in this direction that we should seek the origin of all the taboo phenomena relating to first experiences, for a *Noli me tangere* prohibits human beings from a blinding contact with the real of the 'first time', as is shown in *Life is a Dream*, which is the tragedy of the rejection of the immediate, of the impossibility of acceding to immediacy. Human reality seems able to begin only with the 'second time'. 'A bar for nothing': this is the motto of that life lived at one remove that causes the farmer to sacrifice the first bushel of his harvest, young Romans to sacrifice their first beard to Jupiter, and Carthaginian couples to sacrifice their first-born in honour of the god Baal. The real begins only with the second 'go', which is the truth of human life, bearing the mark of the double; as for the first go, which duplicates nothing, it is precisely a 'free go' ('un coup pour rien'). In short, to be real according to the definition of reality that prevails in *this* world—the double of an inaccessible real—one must copy something. Now, this is never the case with the first go at something, which copies nothing: all that remains, then, is to abandon that one to the gods, who are alone worthy to live under the sign of the unique, alone capable of knowing the joy of firstness. So Talleyrand was right to say that the first was right. But it was so right that it was right only for the gods and it defines the share that is due to them.

Shorn of immediacy, human reality is, quite naturally, also shorn of a *present*. This means that human beings are deprived of reality itself, if we follow the Stoics on this matter, one of whose strongest arguments was that reality could only be conjugated in the present. But the present would be too disquieting if it were merely immediate and primary. It is approachable only by way of re-presentation, in terms, then, of an iterative structure which assimilates it to a past or a future with the aid of a mild temporal offsetting that diminishes its unbearable vigour and permits its assimilation only in the form of a double that is more digestible than the original in its primary rawness. Hence the need for a certain coefficient of 'inattention to life' within attentive, useful perception itself. It is only when this element of inattention is exaggerated that the phenomena of *paramnesia* (false recognition, déjà vu) are produced, as described by Bergson in the study to which we have already referred:

> Suddenly, as one is watching a spectacle or engaged in a conversation, the conviction wells up that one has already seen what one is seeing, already heard what one is hearing, already uttered the sentences one is uttering; that one has been at this same place before and in the same frame of mind—feeling, perceiving, thinking and wishing the same things; that one is, in short, reliving some moments of one's past life down to the very last detail. The illusion is sometimes so complete that, while it

lasts, one believes that one is at any moment about to predict what is going to happen: How could one not already know it, since one feels one is going to *have known* it? It is not unusual at such times to perceive the external world peculiarly, as though in a dream. One becomes estranged from oneself; one is close to feeling split in two and to watching what one says and does as a simple spectator.[6]

Bergson sees these kinds of illusions as 'memories of the present' which abnormally reduplicate current perception:

The memory evoked is a memory hanging in the air without anything in the past on which to base itself. It does not correspond to any previous experience. One knows this, one is convinced of it, and this conviction is not the product of reasoning but is immediate. It is fused with the feeling that the memory evoked must simply be a duplicate of the current perception. Is it, then, a 'memory of the present'? If this is not how it is put, that is surely because the expression would seem contradictory, because one cannot conceive memory other than as a repetition of the past, because one cannot accept that a repetition may bear the mark of the past independently of what it represents and, lastly, because one is being a theorist without realizing it and one believes any memory to be posterior to the perception it reproduces. But something akin to this is being said; there is talk of a past that would seem to be separated from the present by no interval: 'I felt a kind of release within me that eliminated all of the time between that minute in the past and the present minute' [F. Gregh . . .]. Here we have indeed the characteristics of the phenomenon.[7]

Bergson's analysis construes this illusion as a phenomenon of semi-morbid disconnection, an abandonment to that 'luxury memory' that is the memory of the present, whereas the only things useful to current perception are certain memories of the past. There is probably something more general and more normal in this phenomenon of double perception: not just a momentary distraction in respect of the present, characterizing 'the most inoffensive form of inattention to life,'[8] but a *denial of the present* that is already palpable in any normal perception. It should be noted that this denial of the present, which relegates it to the past (or, alternatively, projects it into the future) sometimes occurs in circumstances not at all conducive to 'inattention': circumstances when the situation is grave and the present suddenly becomes openly inassimilable. The automatic rejection of the present into the past or into the future is most often the act of a subject not thinking of something else that has seized his attention but, rather, fascinated by the present matter at hand from which he is desperately trying to distract himself. He succeeds in so doing only by relegating it, as if by magic, to the recent past or the near future, to wherever or whenever he can, provided it is no longer here or in the present—provided it is 'anywhere out of the world', as Charles Baudelaire wrote. Out of pity, a double seems to seek out the subject who is being stifled by the present and that double finds a natural place that is slightly offset—either a little before or a little after—in time. A novel by Alain Robbe-Grillet, *The Erasers* (1968)—ancient in its inspiration since it takes over the Sophoclean theme of the detective who is also the murderer—precisely expresses this rejection of the present and its erratic doubling. In the novel, the event is presented as having already taken place but also as being due to take place: for, while the detective muses on the murder committed the day before, the murderer—who is none other than the 'detective' himself—pictures for himself in advance the murder he is going to commit. A murder for which the real 'hero'—who is ultimately neither detective nor murderer (not yet detective nor already murderer or vice versa)—will provide the temporal site at the end of the novel that rings out as sharply as the gunshot that ends the book: namely, the *present*. But the present is precisely what is not perceived, what is invisible, unbearable; and it is very sincerely that the murderer assures the police he has not committed the murder. For, he says, the crime took place in the present—and I was not there. The past or the future will always be there to *erase* the imperceptible, unbearable vividness of the present. And it is, indeed, also in this sense that a certain philosophy can help us to live: it erases the real and replaces it with a representation. It is in this same sense that Montaigne describes the eternally indigestible character of the real, which lends memories and predictions their advantage: 'A notable example of the wild curiosity of our nature to grasp at and anticipate future things, as if we had not enough to do to digest the present.'[9]

Setting immediacy aside, referring it to another world that provides the key to it, both from the standpoint of its meaning and its reality—this is the metaphysical enterprise par excellence. The versions of that other world may vary but its function—to set aside the immediate—always remains the same: it is the oracular function, which duplicates the event, making it the image of another event of which it is merely a more or less successful imitation, since it is more or less faked. It does, however, happen, rather as in the example of the two Cratyluses, that the imitation is so successful that it can no longer be distinguished from the original, so that the other world is none other than this world, without, however, the idea being abandoned that this world is indeed the copy of that other world, which nonetheless differs from it in no respect at all. This particular version of the other world defines precisely the structure of Hegel's metaphysics, the novel feature of which is that it makes the two worlds coincide, thus obtaining—at the cost of a tautological reiteration—a 'concrete' that is apparently freed from metaphysical illusion, since it already contains in itself all the properties that also define the other world. The dialectic of the unique and its double seems to spin madly here, after the fashion of a confused compass needle. In this, Hegel's subtlety is not 'somewhat empty and forced,' as his commentator Jean Hyppolite writes, but is, rather, very revealing of the madness inherent in the duplication of the unique.[10] Analyzing the concept of force, Hegel distinguishes, overall, between two forms of illusion: the crude illusion, which consists in taking things to be as they appear; and the metaphysical illusion—the one Hegel claims to overcome—which consists in relegating the real into another world entirely distinct from the world of appearance.[11] We must, therefore, distinguish not between two worlds but three. First, there is the world of sensible (or sensuous) appearances; second, the supersensible world insofar as it differs from the sensible world ('the first supersensible world'); and third, that same supersensible world but considered now insofar as it ultimately coincides with the first world of appearances ('the second supersensible world'). This third world, which is opposite to the second insofar as it suppresses the difference which that world claimed to establish between itself and the sensible world, but is not, for all that, as one with the immediate world (this latter being incapable of 'thinking itself' because it has not yet completed the journey of its radical—metaphysical—doubting and the return to itself), is what Hegel calls the 'upside-down' or 'inverted world'.[12] In other words, it is a double of the unique world but a double that is precisely that unique world itself, though not until after it has turned a *somersault* that pulls off the metaphysical trick merely the better to bring us back to the starting point. It is a trick that is not without profit, since we set out from sensible appearances, from the mere outer shell of the real, but, once the somersault is over, we arrive at 'The Interior, or the Bottom of Things.'[13] We discover, then, that the sensible (or sensuous) is no other than the progressive concretization of the supersensible 'beyond', representing what Hegel calls the 'fulfilment' of that beyond, in exactly the same way as the double can, in terms of the oracular structure, be regarded as the realization or 'fulfilment' of the single or unique. Hegel confirms this:

> The inner world, or supersensible beyond, has, however, *come into being*: it *comes from* the world of appearance which has mediated it; in other words, appearance is its essence and, in fact, its filling. The supersensible is the sensuous and the perceived posited as it is *in truth*; but the *truth* of the sensuous and the perceived is to be *appearance*. The supersensible is therefore appearance *qua* appearance.[14]

And his commentator confirms it too:

> [L]et us dwell on what Hegel curiously terms the experience of the 'upside-down world.' It is because the first suprasensous world (the immediate elevation of the sensuous to the intelligible) reverses, or upends, itself in itself that movement is introduced into it and that it is no longer merely a replica of the phenomenon but completely joins the phenomenon which in this way mediates itself in itself and becomes

manifestation of essence. We understand what Hegel meant when he claimed that there were not two worlds but that the intelligible world was 'the phenomenon as phenomenon,'[15] i.e. 'manifestation,' which in its authentic development is only the self-manifestation of self.[16]

That is to say, this world is the other of another world which is, as it happens, the same as this world, for that mysterious route by which the phenomenon mediates itself within itself to become manifestation of essence is no other than the path that leads from A to A by way of A. This strange coincidence of this world and the other world (which simply expresses the coincidence of the unique and its double) does not escape Hegel, who sees it as the last word in the philosophical mystery—the mystery of the fact that things are precisely what they are and not otherwise. Hence the idea—in this case, downright insane—that the real's coincidence with itself is the product of a ruse:

> The great ruse, Hegel wrote in a personal note, is that things are what they are . . . The essence of essence is to manifest itself; manifestation is the manifestation of essence.[17]

This identity of the appearance and the real it conceals is both a ruse of destiny and a godsend for Hegel: it actually provides an eternally satisfying explanation for the invisible character of the other world—a matter liable to trouble the incredulous. The other world is invisible because it so happens that it is doubled by *this* world, which prevents us from seeing it. If this world differed ever so slightly from the supersensible world, that supersensible world would be, so to speak, more tangible: it would be possible to detect it in the very discrepancy that caused it to differ from the sensible (or sensuous) world. But it so happens there is no such discrepancy. The supersensible world is the exact duplicate of the sensible world; it does not differ from it in the slightest. And that is why it is so difficult to perceive: it will always be concealed by its double or, in other words, by the real world. A better hiding place could scarcely be imagined. Hegelian philosophy thus appears as the very essence of oracular thought: it announces the manifestation within the real of another *real* that cannot be doubted since it is already wholly present at the level of the immediately perceived real. And it matters little that this real and this *real* are, in Hegel, one and the same. On the contrary, the rigorous duplication merely embraces more closely that oracular structure whose trick is to have surprise and the satisfaction of expectation coincide in a single event. As we know, this oracular structure characterizes all the philosophies of the nineteenth century. We find a particularly evocative echo of it in J. G. Fichte, who, if Arthur Schopenhauer is to be believed, stubbornly repeated to his students that it is precisely because things are as they are, that they *are* ('Es ist, weil es so ist, wie es ist').

This oracular structure of the real also shows itself in the philosophies of the twentieth century, particularly in certain philosophies that are regarded as avant-garde because they have not yet been compared with past ideas from which they often differ only in form or detail.

For example, the Hegelian structure of the real is plain for all to see in the structure of the real according to Jacques Lacan. It matters little that in Lacan the real is not underpinned, as in Hegel, by another reality but, rather, by a 'signifier' that is 'by nature only symbol of an absence'.[18] What matters is the equal incapacity of the real to account for itself, to supply its own meaning, as in Lucretius; the equal need to look 'elsewhere'—albeit to an 'absence' rather than a 'beyond'—for the key that enables immediate reality to be deciphered. What matters is that meaning is not here but elsewhere. Hence a duplication of the event, which splits into two elements: on one hand, its immediate manifestation and, on the other, what that manifestation manifests or, in other words, its meaning. The meaning is precisely what is provided not by itself but by the other: this is the sense in which metaphysics, which looks for a meaning beyond appearances, has always been a metaphysics of the other. It is the other of the sensible that explains the sensible in Hegel, just as it is the other of the penis (the 'phallus') that gives its meaning to the penis in Lacan. And indeed the similarity is reinforced by a single, strange intuition—in both Hegel and Lacan —that the other being sought in this way is none other than the selfsame. In Hegel, without the supersensible, the sensible has no meaning; hence the supersensible exists—and is, as it so happens, the sensible itself. In Lacan, without the phallus, the penis has no meaning; hence the phallus exists, yet as everyone knows, the phallus is no other than the penis. The oracular structure of ambiguity is the very structure Lacan privileges above all others, as is announced in the 'Seminar on "The Purloined Letter"', in which what is real 'signifies' only insofar as it 'is missing from its place' (just as the event announced by the oracle is, in fact, only expected insofar as it is different).[19] This is how we should understand the meaning of these enigmatic 'L' diagrams—'that are a puzzle to some people,'[20] from which it emerges that the ego is precisely not the ego and that the other, in fact, differs from the other. We find here, once again, the Hegelian structure of tautological iteration, complicated only by the rejection of the signifier into an eternally offset position from the thing it signifies (whereas Hegelian signification ultimately 'fills' the real and coincides with it). Hence, in Lacan, the constant denegation, which inevitably seems obsessive: the penis is the phallus inasmuch as it is not—and vice versa. Being is not being or, rather, it is so only insofar as it is not. White is black only insofar as it is not or, alternatively, only insofar as black is, in fact, white.

These considerations cast an interesting light on the psychological structure of what, since the second half of the nineteenth century, has been known in France as *le chichi*. Of course, *chichi* or affectation is characterized, first of all, by a taste for complication, which itself expresses a distaste for the simple. But, we have to understand the *double meaning* of this rejection of the simple, at the risk of appearing ourselves to succumb to the failing that we are seeking to study from an external vantage point. At a first level, distaste for the simple merely expresses a taste for complication: the complicated manoeuvre is preferred to the simple attitude, even if the goal pursued in each case is the same—and even if this excess of complication may mean missing that goal. At a second level, however, which does not eliminate the first but deepens and elucidates it, distaste for the simple denotes fear in the face of the unique, distance from *the thing itself*, the taste for *complication* expressing in the first instance a need for *duplication* required for the evasive acceptance of a real whose raw uniqueness is instinctively sensed to be indigestible. Understood in this way, this rejection of the simple enables us to understand why the affected engage in their affectation—not so much to seem clever to others as to subdue the lustre of the real, the vividness of which wounds them with its intolerable uniqueness. Things are bearable only if mediated, doubled: there is nothing in this world that can be taken 'just as it is'. This is expressed very clearly by Madelon in Molière's *The Pretentious Young Ladies* (1659), when she tells her father that a man should not 'come out point-blank with a proposal of marriage' and that 'the mere thought of it makes [her] sick at heart'.[21] The sense of the 'point-blank' in this passage ('de but en blanc' in Molière's French) is going straight for the target, aiming directly for the unique or the single without the aid of the double. Complication here is simply a *pis-aller*, a protection against the ineluctability of the unique, to which affectation, be it 'precious' or metaphysical in essence (supposing that these two essences actually differ from one another), will only ever represent a temporary—or at least illusory—obstacle. Temporary if we are talking simply of a transient 'affectation'; at all events illusory, even if it is stubborn and final: for the rejection of the single and unique will never be accompanied by the prehension of a double, so that the pursuit of the double for which the unique has been sacrificed is doomed in any case to failure, since it is the pursuit of the 'nothing' whose 'other' the real is insanely imagined to be. Thus, affectation is related to a very deep anxiety which we may describe in brief as unease at the idea that by accepting that one is as one is, one agrees by the same token that one is *only* that. Uniqueness, in fact, implies both triumph and humiliation: triumph in being the only one in the world, humiliation in being only that only-one—that is to say, in being almost nothing and, presently, nothing at all. Preciosity would like to have triumph without humiliation and it is in this connection that it betrays not just a taste for complication but, more deeply, a distaste for self as something single and unique. This psychological depth of verbal affectation lends substantial impact to a famous passage in Jean de La Bruyère:

> What are you saying? What is that? I don't follow. Would you begin again, please? I'm following even less now. I've got it at last: you are trying to tell me, *Acis*, that it is cold; why don't you say, 'It is cold'? You want to inform me that it is raining or snowing, then say, 'It is raining or it is snowing.' . . . But, you reply, that is very *plain* [*uni*] and very clear.[22]

45

We may note, however, before concluding, that the theme of duplication is not necessarily linked to a metaphysical structure of thinking. Alongside the metaphysical structure of the double, which leads to a depreciation of the real (depriving the immediate of all other realities and emptying the present of all past facts and all future possibilities), we may conceive of a non-metaphysical structure of duplication, which leads, by contrast, to enriching the present with every—future and past—potentiality. This is the theme—at once Stoic and Nietzschean—of the eternal return, which paradoxically loads the present with all the positive features of which metaphysical duplication deprives it, in such a way that the present, the here-and-now, becomes what is full and the elsewhere and the elsewhen are consigned to the place of emptiness to which immediacy was consigned in the opposite perspective. And this occurs through a 'release' quite like that evoked by Gregh when he says, 'I felt a kind of release within me that eliminated all of the time between that minute in the past and the present minute.'[23] This release, whereby the present is rehabilitated by being suddenly enriched with all the positive features of which it was deprived up to that point, probably appears more clearly in poetry than in philosophy—even a philosophy poetic in its affinities, like that of Friedrich Nietzsche. *The Chimeras* (1854) by Gérard de Nerval, to confine ourselves to that one poet, suggests this theme of the duplication of the present in every past and every future but do so only for the glory and the celebration of the present itself. Reiteration, a general theme of *The Chimeras*, redounds here to its own advantage and not to the advantage of what is reiterated. What counts is that everything is forever *first*. The thirteenth time itself will always be the first and only time, as the first two lines of the poem 'Artémis' assert.[24] Nerval's itinerary here is the opposite of the metaphysical: he does not strike out the present in favour of the past or the future but strikes out the past and future to the advantage of the present which finds itself enriched in this way or, better, 'filled', as Hegel would say, with all that has taken place and all that will ever take place. This sense of duplication leads, then, not to a flight from here to elsewhere but to a quasi-magical convergence of every elsewhere on the here-and-now. This convergence, glimpsed by Nerval at the end of his life, defines the *state of grace*. Hence the felicitous character of Nervalian duplication in *The Chimeras* which, far from depriving the present of its specific reality, adds the infinite series of other realities to it. The present is, at every moment, the sum of all presents, and the expression 'present' is to be understood here in its dual meaning of the gift of the moment (the gift of this present) and absolute giving (the gift of every 'present' or, in other words, of all time, *durée*). And the final return to stillness, to that unique state which, at the end of the sonnet 'Delfica', seals the series of all past moments in the present instant alone and does not forget any reality. Indeed, it actually affirms all of them at once, for it brings home with it the totality of all that is, has been and will be, thus endowing every moment of life with all the richness of eternity:

47

Do you know it, DAPHNE, this old romance,
     at the foot of the sycomore or the white
     laurel trees, beneath the olive, the myrtle
     or the trembling willows, this song of love
     . . . that always rebegins!

Do you recognize the TEMPLE with its
     immense peristyle, and the bitter lemons
     that bore the imprint of your teeth? And
     the grotto, fatal to its careless guests, where
     the vanquished dragon's ancient seed lies
     asleep?

They shall return, these gods you still bemoan!
     Time will bring back the order of the an-
     cient days; the earth has shuddered with a
     prophetic breath . . .

Meanwhile the sibyl with the Latin face still
     sleeps beneath the Arch of Constantine
     —and nothing has unsettled the severe
     portico.[25]

Be a friend to the present that is passing: the future
and the past will be given to you *into the bargain*.

Notes

1 Jean-Pierre Attal, *L'image 'métaphysique' et autres essais*
   (The 'Metaphysical' Image and Other Essays) (Paris:
   Gallimard, 1969), p. 178.

2 Plato, *Cratylus*, 432a; Plato, *Parmenides*, 132d.

3 See Vincent Descombes, *Le Platonisme* (Paris: PUF,
   1970), p. 40f.

4   Søren Kierkegaard, 'Repetition' in *Kierkegaard's Writings*, VOL. 6, *Fear and Trembling/Repetition* (Howard V. Hong and Edna H. Hong trans) (Princeton, NJ: Princeton University Press, 1983), pp. 125–232.

5   See Alfred de Vigny, *Oeuvres complète*, VOL. 1 (F. Baldensperger ed.) (Paris: Gallimard, 1950), p. 123–4.

6   Bergson, 'L'Énergie spirituelle', p. 897.

7   Ibid., pp. 921–2. The quote from Fernand Gregh appears in Eugène Bernard Leroy, *L'illusion de fausse reconnaissance: contribution à l'étude des conditions psychologiques de la reconnaissance des souvenirs* (The Illusion of False Recognition: A Contributions to the Study of Psychological Conditions for the Recognition of Memories) (Paris: F. Alcan, 1898), p. 183.

8   Ibid., p. 929.

9   Michel de Montaigne, 'Of Prognostications' (BK 1, CHAP. 11) in *Essays of Montaigne* (Charles Cotton trans., William C. Hazlitt revd) (London: Alex Murray and Son, 1870), p. 39.

10 Jean Hyppolite, *Genesis and Structure of Hegel's Phenomenology of Spirit* (Samuel Cherniak and John Heckman trans) (Evanston, IL: Northwestern University Press, 1974), p. 124.

11 See G. W. F. Hegel, 'Force and the Understanding: Appearance and the Supersensible World' in *Phenomenology of Spirit* (A. V. Millar trans.) (Oxford: Clarendon Press, 1977), pp. 79–103.

12 Ibid., p. 96.

13 Hyppolite, *Genesis and Structure*, p. 125. This 'interior' is rendered as 'inner world' in Millar's translation of Hegel.

14 Hegel, *Phenomenology of Spirit*, p. 89. [Appearance here translates as *Erscheinung*, which is also variously translated as 'phenomenon' and 'manifestation'.—Trans.]

15 'The phenomenon as phenomenon' is an alternative translation of '*Erscheinung als Erscheinung*' from Millar's 'appearance *qua* appearance'.—Trans.

16 Hyppolite, *Genesis and Structure*, p. 125.

17 Ibid. [Translation modified.]

18 Jacques Lacan, 'Le séminaire sur "La Lettre volée"', *Écrits* (Paris: Éditions du Seuil, 1966), pp. 11–61. Available in English as 'Seminar on "The Purloined Letter"' (Jeffrey Mehlman trans.) in John Muller and William Richardson (eds), *The Puloined Poe: Lacan, Derrida and Psychoanalytic Reading* (Baltimore, MD: Johns Hopkins University Press, 1988), pp. 28–54.

19 '[M]anque à sa place'. Lacan, Le séminaire sur "La Lettre volée"', p. 25.

20 '[Q]ui pour certains font casse-tête'. Ibid., p. 42.

21 Molière, *The Pretentious Young Ladies* (Henri Van Laun trans.) (New York: R. Worthington, 1880), p. 225.

22 Jean de La Bruyère, *Les Caractères de Théophraste traduits du grec avec Les Caractères ou les moeurs de ce siècle* (Characters, or the Manners of the Age, with the Characters of Theophrastus) (Paris: Garnier, 1962), p. 153. [Rosset's point is that the detested 'clear' language is a language that is *uni*—literally, 'united', 'made one'.—Trans.]

23 See p. 35 in this volume.

24 'Artémis', the sixth of the sonnets in *Les Chimères* (*The Chimeras*), begins: 'La Treizième revient . . . C'est encor la première; / Et c'est toujours la seule,—ou c'est le seul moment' ('The Thirteenth returns . . . She's again the first; / and still the only one—or the only moment'). See Gérard de Nerval, *Selected Writings* (Richard Sieburth trans., introd. and annot.) (London: Penguin, 1999), p. 368.

25 Ibid., p. 367.

THE PSYCHOLOGICAL ILLUSION:
MAN AND HIS DOUBLE

'"I" IS ANOTHER'

In Plato's *Cratylus*, Socrates shows that the best repro-
duction of Cratylus necessarily implies a difference from
Cratylus: there cannot be two Cratyluses, since each one
would paradoxically have to posses the basic property
of Cratylus, which is to be himself and not someone
else. What characterizes Cratylus, like everything in the
world, is, then, his singularity, his uniqueness. This basic
structure of the real—uniqueness—marks out both its
value and its finitude: everything has the privilege of
being only one, which lends it infinite value, and the dis-
advantage of being irreplaceable, which devalues it infinitely. For the death of the unique is irremediable.
'There's never been another one like him': but once he
is gone, there are none. Such is the ontological fragility
of everything that comes into existence: the uniqueness
of the thing, which constitutes its essence and gives

it its price, is counterbalanced by a disastrous ontological quality—never having more than a very weak, very ephemeral participation in being.

We may, however, imagine the paradoxical situation outlined by Socrates coming to pass (we cannot *conceive* it, since it implies a contradiction, but we can *imagine* conceiving it). There will be two Cratyluses, then, and the one will be the exact double of the other, so that they will not differ in any respect from each other and it will even be impossible to speak about them as 'one' and 'other'. This image, which merely realizes concretely the common fantasy of the duplication of the unique, does, however, present one noteworthy particularity: the unique that is duplicated here is no longer some object or event in the external world but a human being or, in other words, a subject, the self itself. This particular case of the duplication of the unique covers the range of phenomena known as doubling—or, more commonly, *splitting*—of the personality and it has given rise to countless literary works and innumerable commentaries of a philosophical, psychological and, most importantly, psychopathological order, since the splitting of the personality also characterizes the fundamental structure of the most serious forms of madness, such as schizophrenia. The literary theme of the double appears with particular insistence in the nineteenth century (E. T. A. Hoffmann, Adelbert von Chamisso, Edgar Allan Poe, Guy de Maupassant and Fyodor Dostoyevsky are the writers who have most famously depicted it), but its origin is clearly very ancient, since 'doubles' and identical twin brothers occupy an important place in classical theatre, as in Plautus' *Amphitruo* or *The Menaechmi* . Yet the double—in this sense of splitting or doubling of the personality—is not confined only to literary expression: it is also at work in painting and may even be said to be an essential, crucial theme of that art from the psychological standpoint, if it is true, as has been argued, that it is the basic mission of all painters to achieve (or fail to achieve) their 'self-portrait' (and to do so in whatever genre of painting they engage and even in the absence of any attempt to depict their own image on canvas). The double has also been a concern of music, being present, for example, in three major musical works of the early twentieth century, which we shall take here as illustrations: Igor Stravinsky's *Petrushka* (1910–11); Manuel de Falla's *El Amor brujo* (1915), based on a plot by Gregorio Martinez Sierra; and Richard Strauss' *Die Frau ohne Schatten* (premiere 1919) with a libretto by Hugo von Hofmannsthal.

PETRUSHKA: Petrushka is a marionette, the comical double of the real Petrushka who loves the Ballerina, and who can act only *as a double*—that is to say, as the puppet that he is. Murdered by the Moor, another marionette who, out of jealousy, runs him through with his sabre, Petrushka gets back his soul as he dies, thus recovering the *original* which he had, up to that point, been able only to mimic, and it is his real being we suddenly see gesticulating from the rooftop in ghostly fashion, thumbing his nose at his master who runs off as the curtain falls.

EL AMOR BRUJO: The beautiful gypsy, Candelas, loves the young Carmelo. But each time she tries to throw herself into his arms, she sees the ghost of a man she once loved and who continues to torment her even from beyond the grave. A devoted friend, Lucia, agrees to deflect the ghost's attention onto herself. In this way, she frees Candelas who goes to Carmelo and runs off with him as the bells of morning announce the dawn and all the sprites of the night vanish.

DIE FRAU OHNE SCHATTEN: To atone for an offence committed by her father, a princess has been deprived of her shadow and also of fertility: she cannot become a mother. A solution presents itself: to buy a poor woman's shadow, thus depriving her of her fertility. The princess refuses this solution at last, having been moved by the fate that would befall the unfortunate. This moment of compassion is immediately rewarded by a supernatural grace that lifts the curse and restores the princess' shadow and fertility.

Of these three examples, only *Petrushka* presents the theme of splitting/doubling in a simple and immediate form. In *El Amor brujo*, Candelas is not haunted by her double but by the double of the woman she once was, which appears in the ghost of her dead lover. The lover that *she* is today is disturbed by the lover she was in the past but, happily, love in the present ultimately wins out, as in Guillaume Apollinaire's 'Song of the Poorly Loved' (1904) or in another opera by Richard Strauss and Hofmannsthal, *Arianna auf Naxos* (1912). In *Die Frau ohne*

Schatten, the shadow does not represent the double but constitutes, on the contrary, something like its opposite. Here, the shadow symbolizes the materiality and embodiment of the heroine in the uniqueness of a here-and-now and, consequently, her ability to love and reproduce life. As a result, the woman with a shadow, which she becomes at the end of the opera, is a woman freed from the curse of the double—that double which invariably leads to a person's reality being located outside of him- or herself. The woman without a shadow is the woman with a double, for being without a shadow means one is merely a shadow oneself, a shadow corresponding only to the real which one 'doubles' without being able to coincide with it. When the miracle occurs at the end of the piece, that coincidence takes place: having at last become herself, the princess ceases to be anyone's double and recovers her shadow. The move from woman-without-shadow to woman-without-double is nothing less than the return from the other to the self, from elsewhere to here, which marks the recognition of the unique and the acceptance of life.

A famous study by Otto Rank concludes that the splitting/doubling of the personality is connected to the ancestral fear of death.[1] The double the subject evokes for himself is said to be an immortal double, whose task is to afford the subject protection from his own death. The superficiality of the diagnosis results here from the fact that Rank has not grasped the real hierarchy which connects the unique individual to his 'double' in the splitting of personality. It is true that the double is always intuitively understood as having a 'better' reality than the subject himself—and, in this sense, he may seem to represent a kind of immortal dimension by comparison with the mortality of the subject. But, much rather than his imminent death, the source of the subject's anxiety is his non-reality, his non-existence. It would not be so bad to die if one could at least be certain one had lived. Now, what the subject comes to doubt, in the splitting of the personality, is *this life itself,* however perishable it may be in other ways. In the baneful couple formed by the union of the self with a ghostly other, it is not the self that possesses the reality, but the ghost: it isn't the other who is my double, *but I who am the other's double*. His is the reality, mine the shadow. In the words of Arthur Rimbaud, 'I' is 'someone else'; 'real life' is 'absent'. Similarly, in Maupassant, *Lui* or *Le Horla* are not shadows of the writer but the real, genuine writer whom Maupassant merely apes pitifully: it is not *he* who imitates me, but I who imitate *him* [*Lui*]. The real, in this kind of disturbance, is always on the other's side. And the worst mistake, for the person haunted by the one he takes to be his double—yet who is in reality the original he is himself duplicating—would be to try to kill his 'double'. In killing him, he kills himself, or rather he kills the person he was trying desperately to be, as Poe says so well at the end of 'William Wilson' (1839) when the unique individual (apparently the double of Wilson) has died at the hands of his double (who is the narrator himself):

> You have conquered, and I yield. Yet, henceforward art thou also dead—dead to the World,

to Heaven and to Hope! In me didst thou exist
—and, in my death, see by this image, which is
thine own, how utterly thou hast murdered
thyself.[2]

The solution to the psychological problem posed by
the splitting of the personality does not lie, then, in my
mortality, which is in any case certain, but in my existence, which here seems dubious. Who am I, who claim
to *be*—and, moreover, claim to *be me*—basing myself in
this way on that 'false obviousness which the self draws
on to parade existence'?[3] It is not enough to say I am
unique, as is everything in the world. Looking at this
more closely, I have the privilege—which is also perhaps
a curse—of being unique on two counts, since I am this
particular—'unique'—case in which the unique cannot
be *seen*. I am well aware of the uniqueness of all the
things around me and proclaim it without being greatly
pressed to do so: this is because it is, at least, vouchsafed
to me to see it, to posit it as a thing I can observe or mani-
pulate. It is not the same with me, whom I have never
seen and shall never see, even in a mirror. For the mirror
is deceptive and provides a 'false self-evidence' or, in
other words, an illusion of seeing: it does not show me
but a reverse me, an other; it does not show my body but
a surface, a reflection. It is, when all is said and done, just
a last chance to apprehend me, which will always end up
disappointing me, whatever jubilation I may have felt at
the age of 10 months when I understood (but did not
see) that this image moving about in front of me bore
some vague relation to my person. This is why the quest

for the self, particularly in dissociative (or 'splitting') disorders, is always linked to a kind of obstinate return to the mirror and to everything that bears some similarity to mirrors—such as the obsession with symmetry in all its forms—that, in its way, repeats the impossibility of ever rendering this invisible thing one is trying to see, which might be said to be the self 'live'—or another self, its exact double. Symmetry is itself like the mirror: what it produces is not the thing itself but its other, its reverse, its opposite, its projection about some axis or on some plane. The fate of the vampire, whose image—even inverted—is not reflected in mirrors, here symbolizes the fate of everyone and everything: the fate of not being able to experience one's existence with the aid of a *real doubling* of the unique, and hence of existing only problematically. Ultimately, the true misfortune in the splitting of the personality is never to be able really to split or double oneself: the person haunted by the double lacks a double. The acceptance of the self by the self thus has as its basic precondition the renunciation of the double, the abandonment of the project of having the self apprehend itself in a contradictory duplication of the unique. Hence, the pyschologically succesful rendering of the self-portrait, for painters, implies abandoning self-portraiture itself, as is the case with Johannes Vermeer, one of whose profound secrets was to represent himself from behind in the famous *Painter in his Studio* (1666).[4]

The 'narcissistic wound', which is so conducive to what is called an actor's temperament, lies here: in doubt of oneself, from which one is freed only by reiterated reinforcement from the other—in this case, the audience.

We know that the spectacle of the split personality in others—a theme copiously illustrated in horror films and novels—is an experience that exerts an assured terrorizing effect. We thought we were dealing with the original but, in fact, we had only ever seen his deceptive, reassuring double; suddenly, here is the original in person, sniggering and revealing himself both as the other and as the 'real one'. Perhaps the basis of the anxiety, apparently linked here to the mere discovery that the visible other was not the real other, is to be sought in a deeper terror: that I am not, myself, the person I thought I was. And, even more deeply, that I suspect, on this occasion, that I am perhaps not something, but nothing.

The connection between horror and the double can be seen in exemplary fashion in a famous film by Alberto Cavalcanti, *Dead of Night* (1945). All the events in that film are presented as having already vaguely taken place ('false recognition') and it is only at the end that the spectator discovers with dread that what he has been shown as repeating an elusive, dream-like past was, in fact, a premonition of an imminent future: the present is scattered along the dual axes of past and future, while the real collapses vertiginously, coming, as it does, to lack any *here* and *now*. Moreover, a remarkable episode in the film stages the encounter between human being and double: the sequence involving a ventriloquist grappling with his dummy, who increasingly slides out of his master's control and appropriates his reality. It is a hallucinatory scene of schizophrenic splitting in which a man dies suffocated by his double, devoured by his own image.

The recognition of self, which already implies a paradox (since it involves grasping that which is precisely impossible to grasp, and since 'taking control' of oneself resides paradoxically in renouncing that control), also necessarily implies an exorcism: it implies exorcizing the double that poses an obstacle to the existence of the unique and demands that the unique be something other than simply itself and nothing but itself. There should be no self that is simply self, no here that is simply here, no now that is simply now—this is the exigency imposed by the double, which demands a little more and is ready to sacrifice all that exists (in other words, the unique) for all the rest or, in other words, for all that does not exist. And this rejection of the unique is merely one of the most general forms of the rejection of life. This is why the elimination of the double heralds the resurgence of the real and merges into the joy of an entirely new morning, like the one rung out so joyfully by the bells at the end of *El Amor brujo*. By chasing away the spectre of the double, the kindly Lucia has dispelled the evils of the night, the central one being the concealment of the real beneath the unreal by hiding the unique behind its double. The veil is lifted here, enabling Candelas at last to celebrate, as day breaks, the happy reunion of *self with self*.

And this coincidence of self with self always pre-vails in the end, though not always as joyfully. The return of self to self takes paths that are often even more complicated than the artifices deployed by Can-delas to protect himself from his double. It is certain we cannot escape the destiny that makes the self the self and the unique the unique. One will, then, be oneself, come what may. But two routes are possible here: the simple one, which consists in accepting things—or even rejoicing in them—and the complicated one, which con-sists in rejecting them and yet going back over them with redoubled intensity, in conformity with the old Stoic adage 'fata volentem ducunt, nolentem trahunt' (The Fates lead the willing and drag the unwilling). If one takes the second route, one will attempt to avoid the coincidence of self with self by an evasive manoeu-vre not unlike those conveyed in oracular literature, the general fate of which is to hasten the event. In this way, the evasion will highlight the mistake one was try-ing to avoid or at least hide; more exactly, it will create it from whole cloth, the way Oedipus manufactures his fate out of the efforts by which he strives to escape it. It is by refusing to be the 'this' or the 'that' which one is—or refusing to seem to be so in the eyes of others—that one becomes precisely the 'this' or the 'that' and appears such in the eyes of others. There is nothing more 'preachy' than trying to show that one is not, to cite just one example—though this is already one too many, for there is no question here of belittling anyone. The important point is simply that the quality one is seeking to hide or deny by distancing oneself from it is precisely constituted by that distance itself, a distance which contributes, moreover, to making that quality forever invisible to the eyes of its possessor. How could I be such-and-such, when I have spent my whole life distancing myself from it?

The distancing of oneself by oneself, which leads to one being confirmed forever in one's self, can also be felt in the distancing of others, as soon as it appears that those others are both undesirable and like oneself. This is the case, in particular, with certain major dramatic characters. Whoever on the stage appears too like the self one has decided not to be will himself be immediately *split into two*, following the structure of duplication that has already, as we believe, proved its worth where the ego is concerned: in place of the theatrical figure as he actually is, another character appears who banishes the annoyingly similar person to a kind of magical exteriority, from which the ego no longer has anything to fear, not having any relationship with that person. Tartuffe, for example, is not here, but elsewhere; he is neither you nor I but another: this is what we mean when we say that he is not sincere but *hypocritical*. In the same way, the state prosecutor Maillard in Marcel Aymé's *Other People's Heads* (1952) is not at all the banal 'nice man' that he clearly seems to be, but a grotesque crook or, alternatively, a *salaud*, to draw inspiration here from the Sartrean diagnosis, which is interesting in that it provides quite a good illustration of the inevitability which, willy-nilly, condemns to resemblance just those people who most strive not to resemble—the author of *Being and Nothingness* (1943) precisely sharing with Prosecutor Maillard the basic property of being a 'nice man'.

The spectacle of blindness in another person—of his assuredness of being elsewhere, when he is, in fact, *here*; of his certainty of having avoided an undesirable self when he has done no such thing—is a source both of comic delight and mild psychological anxiety. The natural tendency would be to open one's mouth and point out such a manifest error. To say: you are wrong; the double you have produced for yourself is just an unfortunate repetition of your uniqueness and does, indeed, aggravate its unpleasant character; the point is that you would be forgiven for being undesirable—that is to say, for being yourself—were it not for the further buffoonery of taking yourself for someone you are not. But all this is to forget that one makes oneself undesirable only by working at not being so, and that asking others to agree that they are undesirable amounts to attempting to put an end to their undesirability itself. For 'being oneself' here coincides with 'taking oneself for someone else', with the result that, while I believe I am criticizing someone's posturing, it is himself in person that I am criticizing. In showing him that he is other than he believes, I am secretly hoping he is different from what he is, confusedly conceiving that he might indeed be not himself but, actually, someone else. My warning could therefore be said to be as illusory as the illusion it is criticizing. In pressing it, I would merely be succumbing to the illusion of a duplication of the unique at the very point when I am claiming to identify that illusion in the other person and bemoan it. In this way, I fall into the trap I was trying to point out to him.[5] It is here, in an obviousness so tautological that it does not always appear, that the parable of the mote and the beam assumes its essential meaning—rather than in the half-baked 'moral' that is usually drawn from it.

This fantasy of being someone else quite naturally ends at death, since it is I who die and not my double: Blaise Pascal's celebrated phrase 'We shall die alone' designates clearly this irreducible uniqueness of beings in the face of death, even if that was not what he principally had in mind. Death means the end of any possible distance, spatial or temporal, between self and self, and an urgent coincidence with oneself. It is here that Rank's argument assumes profound meaning as, even more, does André Ruellan's proverbial statement in his *Manuel du savoir-mourir* (1963): 'Death is an appointment with oneself: you have to be punctual at least once.'[6]

There is, however, a way of missing this last appointment even while rushing headlong towards it. It is the way recounted by Stephane Mallarmé in the first of his *Contes indiens* (1878), which is both one of the most curious stories about a double and the most perfect illustration of the oracular structure that exists. The impossibility of being both one thing and another, both oneself and someone else is the main subject of this cruel tale, its cruelty lying paradoxically in its very success since, in winning one thing, one necessarily loses another. An ageing king is yearning for his lost youth:

Why can he not be young again? Why does he not look like this handsome young man whose portrait the queen has shown him? And he is deluded into believing that the transformation is possible with the aid of magic. The portrait is said to be enchanted and the king can identify himself with it simply by contemplating it intensely at an initiation ceremony, the details of which the magicians will communicate to him through the queen. When the moment comes, the original of the portrait—that is, the queen's flesh-and-blood lover—appears, having here found a way to substitute himself with impunity for the monarch he has assassinated overnight:

> With a swift blow from his scimitar, he ran the wretched man through, after the latter had perhaps believed for a brief moment in the dazzling accomplishment of his metamorphosis: at least this is what, out of charity, was supposed by the man the tyrant mistook for the spectre of his imminent handsomeness, and who was, in fact, the hero himself.[7]

The oracular structure is reduced to its simplest expression here by way of an ironic short cut that leads directly from the thing one wishes to avoid to the thing one wishes to obtain, since *they are the same*. The event has occurred as desired and announced: 'I' has become 'another' and the monarch, restored to his pristine state, is endowed with all the qualities hoped for from the transformation: he is young, kind and handsome. The enchanted voyage that leads from the one to the other, from the unique to its double, has reached its appointed end but, in the interim, the voyager has died.

Yet, the trick was almost pulled off. The new king falls short in only one tiny respect—he has failed to remain himself while becoming someone else. He simply lacks a little memory to guarantee continuity from the unique to its double, a little of that memory which G. W. Leibniz describes, in his *Discourse on Metaphysics* (1686), as an integral and necessary part of substance, since 'the immortality we require implies memory.'[8] And Leibniz illustrates this definition of the unique with a Chinese story which might have been used as an epigraph to Mallarmé's story and which will serve us here as an epilogue:

> Suppose that someone could suddenly become the king of China, but only on condition of forgetting what he had been, as if he had just been born all over again. Would it not in practice, or in terms of perceivable effects, be the same as if he had been annihilated, and a king of China had been created at the same instant in his place? And that is something which that individual could have no reason to want.[9]

This means that all that is is one and there is no double of the unique: it means that, every other option being excluded, we must, therefore, resolve to be 'particular' or not to be at all.

The security into which the victim of a prophecy retreats is similar to the security relied upon by the individual who tries to find an alternative persona in another person and a way out of the fate that dooms him to be himself: in both cases, security is a trap that completes the binding of the tragic hero to his destiny and his locking of himself up within himself. The finding of shelter and the evasion are expressed in an act that constitutes precisely the damage from which one was trying to protect oneself, conjuring it up from scratch. It is in attempting to avoid killing his father that Oedipus rushes down the path of murder: it is in attempting at all costs to be someone else that people usually confirm that they are themselves, with the result that the place where the evader of destiny finds security is the exact site of his perdition. The apparent 'elsewhere' is simply the 'here' one thought one had moved away from, and the protection one was counting on turns out to be exactly what has precipitated one's doom—like the fisherman's timepiece in Poe's 'A Descent into the Maelström' (1841), which was to have indicated the dangerous hour of the tide and is seen, too late, to have stopped at seven o'clock. False security is more than the ally of illusion; it is its very substance and is at the heart of illusion itself, as Hecate says in Macbeth: '[S]ecurity / is mortals' chiefest enemy.'[10]

This illusory security is also characteristic of a phenomenon related to, but distinct from, illusion—namely, stupidity. More exactly, it characterizes a certain form of stupidity, casting light on both its mechanism and its unassailable vigour.

Stupidity may, in general, be considered from two points of view: its content and its form. The question of the content of stupidity poses an apparently insoluble problem of enumeration that is unrelated to the problematic of the unique and its double. We may content ourselves here, then, with describing the *content* of stupidity summarily as any manifestation of attachment to derisory themes, these latter being inexhaustible in their number and variety. However, given identical content, stupidity may take two rather different *forms*, depending on whether adherence to the derisory theme is immediate and spontaneous or occurs only in a deferred, reflective manner. In the former case, the theme is accepted from the outset on the basis of heredity or cultural environment, without the general problem of stupidity arising—or, in other words, the question of whether or not the theme is intelligent. This is *first-degree stupidity*, unreflected and spontaneous. In the latter case, the theme is accepted only after mature reflection; in other words, the problem of stupidity has been carefully considered and apparently solved—at least from the point of view of the person concerned—since the chosen theme has been selected only after a most severe criticial examination, so that it seems definitively beyond criticism. This is *second-degree stupidity*, internalized and reflexive. In this second form of stupidity, one has taken the problem of stupidity into consideration;

one knows one must avoid being stupid and, in the light of that scrupulous regard, one has chosen an 'intelligent' attitude. Of course, this attitude is nothing but stupidity personified. Paraphrasing Hegel, we might call it 'stupidity become conscious of itself,' though not in the sense of being conscious of being stupid, but conscious, rather, of being intelligent, of constituting a higher region of lucidity to contrast with the background of previously threatening stupidity from which it now feels liberated once and for all.

This second-degree stupidity, the prerogative of persons generally considered intelligent and cultivated (and rightly so), is obviously incurable. In this regard, it represents a form of absolute stupidity, unlike the first-degree form. We may always hope that that form, immediate and spontaneous as it is, has a potential for intelligence: we can imagine it being overcome one day by means of some more or less hypothetical acquisition of awareness. Such hope is vain in the case of the second form of stupidity, since the acquisition of awareness *has already happened*. In this way, confirmed imbecility finds itself in an impasse not unlike that affecting illusion: it is incurable from having reasoned too well, just as Boubouroche in Courteline's play was incurable for having *seen* too well. The last barrier protecting the person from an irrevocable decision has been broken down, like a last headland one has overshot or a last chance one has let slip.

The analogy between this incurable form of stupidity and the oracular or psychological structure of evasion is clear. In the same way as Oedipus or anyone else meets up as a result of having tried to avoid each other, stupidity establishes itself permanently as a result of trying to escape stupidity: it becomes stupid out of a fear of being stupid or, to put it more simply, it becomes itself from having tried to become something else. There is the same illusion of security in the two, linked to a similar confusion between here and elsewhere: I imagine stupidity to be forever distant and a certain intelligence to be present here, whereas stupidity is here and intelligence elsewhere—forever. This inevitable fate also applies to snobbery and, generally, to all who, doubting themselves, endeavour to seek salvation in a *model*: another magic which I hope will make me escape my fate, whereas it shuts me up inexorably in myself.

THE ABANDONMENT OF THE DOUBLE AND THE RETURN TO SELF

One of the characteristics of the art of Vermeer—and perhaps of all art that has reached a certain degree of nobility—is to paint things, not events. The world Vermeer perceives is not the world—forever silent—of insignificant events but that of matter—eternally rich and living. In that world, we might say that the anecdotal has driven out the anecdotal: the chance occurrence of a moment in the day, in a room where nothing important is happening, appears as the essential core of a 'real' in which the apparently notable events, in fact, represent only the subordinate part. From this 'real' apprehended by Vermeer, the ego is absent, for the ego is merely one event among others, being, like them, silent and insignificant. There is, moreover, no self-portrait by Vermeer and the biography we have of the painter runs only to 10 trivial lines. He does, however, seem to have painted himself once, employing a double mirroring effect, in a canvas with no precise name that is known today as *Painter in his Studio*.[11] But he depicted himself from behind, like some nondescript painter, who might be any other person busying himself with his canvas. There is nothing in the costume, size or attitude of the painter that might be regarded as a distinctive sign, nothing then to show any indulgence on the part of the painter towards his person. At the same time, this 'studio' picture—like all Vermeer's canvasses—seems endowed with an intense joy of existence that shines out from it, grabbing the spectator from the outset and attesting to a perpetual jubilation at the spectacle of things. Judging by this moment of felicity, one is easily persuaded that, although the painter captured only a single moment of his joy on the canvas, he could happily have done the same for the preceding or following moment. Only lack of time prevented him from celebrating every moment and every thing.

It would certainly be going too far to see this joy as deriving simply from the abandonment of one's specificity, from the discovery that the ego, as singular being, not only does not interest anyone else but does not even interest myself, who stand only to gain from being spared an image of myself. This indifference to oneself is more effect than cause here: it indicates, rather than gives rise to, a sense of bliss. But the connection between enjoyment of life and indifference to self is manifest here nonetheless. The painter of the *Painter in his Studio* has, in a sense, made visible the invisible: in it, he has painted his absence, which is rendered better this way than if he had simply contented himself with eschewing any form of self-portrait. When nothing is said, it is always possible to imagine some ulterior motive. That is not the case here, for the 'nothing' is said out loud and is displayed in full view on the canvas. Or if not the 'nothing', at least a 'very little', a 'nothing noteworthy'.

Considered from another standpoint, what Vermeer paints in the *Painter in his Studio* is also the mark of a plenitude, which explains the serene, jubilatory atmosphere of the work. This is the very plenitude Candelas experiences at the end of *El Amor brujo*: the reconciliation of self with self, which has the exorcism of the double as its precondition. Not to paint oneself from the front equates to abandoning seeing oneself or, in other words, to abandoning the idea that the self can be perceived in a replica that enables the subject to apprehend himself. The double, which would permit of such an apprehension, would also signify the murder of the subject and the renunciation of self, perpetually relinquishing itself in favour of a ghostly, cruel double. This is cruel for *not being*, as Henry de Montherlant says, for it is ghosts that are cruel; with realities, one can always come to some accommodation. This is why the jubilatory assumption of oneself, the genuine presence of self to self, necessarily implies renunciation of the spectacle of one's image. For the image here kills the model. And the mortal error of narcissism is not, ultimately, to wish to love oneself to excess but, rather, at the moment of choosing between oneself and one's double, to accord preference to the image. The narcissist suffers from not loving himself: he loves only his representation. Truly loving oneself implies an indifference to all copies of oneself as they may appear to others and (by way of others, if I lend too much attention to them) to myself. This is the pitiful secret of Narcissus: an exaggerated attention *to others*. It is, moreover, why he is incapable of loving anyone—either others or himself—love being too important a matter to entrust to others to decide. What does it matter to you if I love you, asked Goethe. This holds only if one agrees implicitly that the assent of another is equally optional in the love one feels for oneself: What does it matter to you if I love me?

The painter of the *Painter in the Studio* is already freed from the burden that Candelas throws off at the end of *El Amor brujo*—the burden of his self-image. This is an escape from the double, an abandonment of his image in favour of the self as such or, in other words, the self as something invisible, unnoticeable and lovable only blindly, as is the case with any love.

Curiously, the obsession with the double in Romantic literature betrays an exactly opposing concern. There

73

the loss of the double, the reflection or the shadow is not a liberation but a baneful effect: the man who has lost his reflection—among myriad others, the hero of a famous tale by Hoffmann—isn't saved but doomed.[12] Far from working to slough off his image, to regard it as a cumbrous, paralyzing burden, the Romantic hero puts his whole being into it and, ultimately, lives only insofar as his life is guaranteed by the visibility of his reflection, a reflection whose extinction would spell death. He is thus perpetually striving after an unfindable double, which he relies on to underwrite his being: if that reflection disappears, the hero dies, as at the end of Poe's 'William Wilson'. The anguished Romantic appears, then—at least in all those texts in which the double is in play—as essentially mistrustful of himself: at all costs he needs external attestation, needs something tangible and visible to reconcile him with himself. Alone, he is nothing. If a double no longer underwrites his being, he ceases to exist.

We may tell this anguished individual that he will find the reflection of himself he is looking for not in a mirror or a faithful duplicate but in the legal documents that establish his identity. He will reply that this is but paltry confirmation, for he wants a flesh-and-blood image, not a presumption of being based on conventional papers that are both perishable and endlessly falsifiable. That is, however, to ask too much, for it so happens that the only half-solid image of oneself one can find resides in documents and in documents alone. The Greek Sophists had, it seems, understood quite profoundly that only institutions—and not some hypothetical 'Nature'—are able to give body and existence to what Plato and Aristotle would conceive as 'substances': the individual will be social or he will not exist at all; it is society and its conventions that will make the phenomenon of individuality possible. What guarantees identity is, and always has been, a public act: a birth certificate, an identity card, the corroborating testimony of one's concierge and neighbours. The human person, conceived as singularity, is thus perceptible to itself only as a 'moral person' in the legal sense of the term: that is to say, not as a substance that can be circumscribed and defined but as an institutional entity guaranteed by the public-records office and the public-records office alone. This means that the human person exists only *on paper* in all senses of the expression: it exists, but it exists 'on paper'; it is noticeable from the outside only theoretically, as a more or less plausible possibility. It is easy to recognize the limits of this plausibility when a number of experiences occur: namely, every time, following some sort of incident or crisis, one is unable to establish one's identity. If you have no papers, it is useless to shout out that you are yourself: this tells no one anything, as is shown in a short play by Courteline entitled *The Registered Letter* (1897).[13]

In it, a post-office clerk recognizes a man who has come to pick up a registered letter as an old acquaintance of his: they engage in conversation, evoke some shared memories and then the customer asks for his letter. But the clerk will not play ball: to take the letter, the customer must prove his identity. This is an absurd devotion to regulations, observes the customer, but the clerk retorts, 'As a man of the world, I recognized you but, as a civil servant, I don't know who you are.' The customer then presents various documents which are recognized as authentic by the clerk. Each time, however, some small detail leaves room for potential doubt and the decision cannot be made. The letter will remain ultimately in the hands of the postal clerk, until such point as his friend has demonstrated beyond question that he is definitely himself and not someone else.

That demonstration is impossible, since the stubborn clerk is, in fact, asking for nothing less than a duplicate of what is unique. Beneath the satire of bureaucratic formalism, we can hear the muffled echo of a deeper anxiety that bears not just on legal but on existential identity: Am I me? Is it I who am alive, despite the lack of papers to underwrite my existence which this scrupulous clerk has just pointed out to me? To be entirely confident of this, I would need a duplicate self which is just what I do not have—and never shall. I am right, then, to doubt myself and, in my incapacity to duplicate myself, I find serious grounds to call myself into question—not just in respect of the ephemeral, fragile character of my existence but in respect of that existence itself, whether or not it happens to be fragile and ephemeral. The anxiety at having no double to take as a template for one's being is not linked fundamentally, as Rank thinks, to the anxiety at having to die (once again, that argument is correct but superficial, for the fear of dying is only a secondary consequence of the fear of not living) but to the deeper anxiety that comes of doubting one's existence. If I need a double to attest to my being and if the only available double is a paper one, then I must conclude that my being is a thing of paper. Or, alternatively, that I have a soul made of paper, as Michel Tournier imagines, when he recounts a bizarre fable on this theme in *The Ogre* (1970).[14]

In that fable, a certain benefactor of humanity, who needed to destroy a troublesome file about himself at police headquarters, set about burning—for philanthropic motives—all the files, records and archives in all the public buildings: city halls, town halls and police stations. Once the last file had been burnt, he observed that humanity had degenerated: people could no longer speak, they went about on all fours, sniffing the ground with their snouts. Our philanthropist was astonished at this but finally 'realized that, in his attempt to free mankind, he had reduced it to the level of animals. And this because *the human soul is made of paper.'*

It is precisely this that the Romantic hero senses and fears: do not burn my double, for I am nothing other and exist only on paper. To burn the double is, at the same time, to burn the unique. This is, in a certain sense, a justified fear—not because the individual is a paper creature but because he is unable to make himself visible—as a unique individual—anywhere other than on paper. The anxiety at seeing one's reflection disappear is thus linked to the anxiety at knowing that one is incapable of establishing one's existence by oneself:

the final proof, the proof *by the thing itself*, which one thought one had up one's sleeve as a decisive trump card, is not and can never be effective. The evidence or arguments one is advancing are intended to establish the fact, but it so happens, by chance and good fortune, that one is able to *show* the thing one was trying so fiendishly hard to demonstrate. And yet one's interlocutor remains completely unmoved. However, I don't try to persuade him; I simply point the thing out. For example, he refuses to accept that Corsica is visible from the mainland on a clear day. After trying every argument I know, I take him up to the hills above Nice and show him Corsica: he sniggers and requests that I be more serious about the problem. A nightmarish dialogue, akin to that of Pascal presenting his 'free thinker' not with arguments in favour of the God of Abraham and Jacob but with that God in person, visible and radiant, only to find that his interlocutor still withheld his assent.

This is why all reasonable thought necessarily halts in the conduct of its argument as soon as *the thing itself* is arrived at. Aristotle and Descartes call this moment by the same name: evidence, the directly visible—without assistance from or mediation by reasoning. There is a moment when we come to the end of proofs and run up against the thing itself, which can only be under-written by itself. This is the moment when the talking stops and philosophy breaks off: adveniente re, cessat argumentum.

There is, however, a domain where the argument does not stop, because the thing itself never shows itself.

And this is precisely my domain: my *self*, my singularity. I cannot rationally stop at myself because I am not visible. If I follow Aristotle on this point, I can no doubt decide that I am a *human being*. On the other hand, I cannot successfully conceive that I am *a* human being in the sense of the precise one that I am. The idea that I am myself is just a vague—though insistent—assumption: a 'strong impression', as Hume has it. And Montaigne: 'All we perform is no other than a Cento, as a man may say, of several pieces.'[15] And Shakespeare: 'We are such stuff / As dreams are made on'[16]—dreams whose stuff is itself of paper: if paper comes up short, as in Courteline's story, then the dream melts away.

A solution, in this desperate case, consists in clinging on to the paper: since my personhood is in doubt, then at least let the documents that attest to it be staunchly resilient. This is the opposite solution to Vermeer's, who abandons the ego in favour of the world. In this case, one is abandoning the world in favour of the ego—and a paper ego at that. The double will efface the original. This is more or less what Plato means by the myth of Theuth:[17] the written memory will supplant the living memory, a solid piece of paper being worth more, in some people's eyes, than an uncertain life. Despairing of ever being oneself—not without reason in some cases—one thus becomes a man of paper, victim of the accursed invention of the god Theuth. The written trace serves as a double by which to gauge one's being—or, rather, one's lack of it. It is in this same way that one becomes ridiculous in Bergson's sense of the term: through never saying anything new but always repeating oneself, in pursuit of an improbable 'template'. Anxiety at being nothing—or almost nothing—quickly leads to absolutely nothing. In this case, Jankélévitch's 'I don't know what' and his 'almost nothing' become 'I don't know' and 'nothing at all'. Especially as, in forcing myself to repeat an ego whose model I would seek in vain, I am condemning myself to repeat the other: and that other, which I gloss in this way, is itself merely the reflection of an absence. A play of interminable resonances, in which the echo of an incapacity to say 'I'— an inability to experience oneself as something—is repeated to infinity. This might be said to be the essence of the contemporary intellectual's misfortune, if François Wahl is to be believed. He calls to mind Jacques Derrida when he writes of 'repetition as the absence forever of any true present.'[18]

This is a profound phrase once it has been shortened and radicalized. For repetition is *always* the absence forever of any present. He who repeats says nothing or, in other words, is not even in a position to repeat himself. The original must do without any image: If I cannot find myself in myself, how much less will I find myself in my echo? The self has to suffice, then, however flimsy it seems or is, since the choice before us is exclusively between the unique, which is very little, and its double, which is nothing. This is what everyday French expresses wonderfully, without realizing it, when it declares that 'on ne se *refait* pas'—you can't change who you are (literally: one does not *remake* oneself).

Notes

1 Otto Rank, *The Double: A Psychoanalytic Study* (Chapel Hill, NC: University of North Carolina Press, 1971).

2 Edgar Allan Poe, *The Complete Stories* (New York: Alfred A. Knopf, 1993), p. 418.

3 These words are taken from the blurb to the original French edition of Lacan's *Écrits*.

4 See Magdeleine Mocquot, 'Vermeer et le portrait en double miroir', *Club français de la Médaille* 18 (1968).

5 These remarks seem to me to provide a (doubtless partial) solution to the problem posed by the character— at once enigmatic and absurd—of the anger that may come over anyone when confronted with a person regarded as stupid or a remark that appears inept. This is a question which attracted the attention of both Montaigne ('Of the Art of Conferring' [BK 3, CHAP. 8] in *Essays*, pp. 539–54) and Blaise Pascal (his famous aphorism on the 'lame man' and the 'lame mind'. See Blasie Pascal, 'Fragment 98' in *Pensées* [Harmondsworth: Penguin, 1966], p. 55). They explain this anger by our inability to prove to the other person that he is wrong, from which follows the impossibility of proving to oneself that one is right. I think it also involves the confused sense that another person could be different from what he is and think differently from what he does, thus illustrating the virtually irresistible force of the fantasy of the double. This anger is ultimately merely one expression among others of the rejection of reality.

6 See André Ruellan, *Manuel du Savoir-Mourir* (Manual of How to Die) (Paris: Pierre Horay, 1963).

7 Stéphane Mallarmé, 'Le portrait enchanté' (The Enchanted Portrait) in *Oeuvres complètes* (Paris: Gallimard, 1945), pp. 595–6.

8   G. W. Leibniz, *Philosophical Texts* (R. S. Woolhouse and Richard Francks eds and trans) (Oxford and New York: Oxford University Press, 1998), p. 86.

9   Ibid.

10 Shakespeare, *Macbeth*, 3.5.32–3.

11 See above, p. 59 and note. See D. Hannema, *Over Johannes Vermeer van Delft* (Heino: De Stuers Foundation, 1972).

12 See E. T. A. Hoffmann, 'A New Year's Eve Adventure' (Alfred Packer trans.) in *The Best Tales of Hoffmann* (E. F. Bleiler ed. and introd.) (New York: Dover Publications, 1967), pp. 104–29.

13 See Georges Courteline, *The Registered Letter* (Jacques Barzun trans.), *The Tulane Drama Review* 3(1) (October 1958): 61–2.

14 Michel Tournier, *The Ogre* (Barbara Bray trans.) (Baltimore, MD: Johns Hopkins University Press, 1997), pp. 38–9. [The italics are in Tournier's original French, though they are omitted from the English edition.—Trans.]

15 Montaigne, 'Of the Inconstancy of our Actions' (BK 2, CHAP. 1) in *Essays*, p. 215. ['Cento' derives from the Latin for a garment of patchwork.—Trans.]

16 William Shakespeare, *The Tempest*, 4.1.156–7.

17 Plato, *Phaedrus*, 274f.; Plato, *Philebus*, 18.

18 François Wahl, *Qu'est-ce que le structuralisme?* (Paris: Seuil, 1968), p. 431.

CONCLUSION

The various aspects of illusion described so far refer to a single function, a single structure, a single failure. The function is to protect from the real; the structure does not involve refusing to perceive the real but, rather, splitting it in two; the failure lies in recognizing the protective double too late as the very reality from which one thought one had found protection. This is the curse of evasion: by way of a phantasmatic duplication, it sends us back to the undesirable starting point, the real. We can see now why evasion is *always* a mistake: it is always inoperative, because the real is always right. We may, admittedly, try to protect ourselves from a future event, if that happens to be possible; we shall never protect ourselves from a past or present event or one that is 'certain to come to pass', as in the oracular symbolics which announces in advance an ineluctable necessity that already has all the characteristics of a present necessity. And the act by which one attempts to slough off that necessity will never be able to 'do any better' than literally reproduce the feared event or, even more exactly, constitute that event. This is what happens to Oedipus, as it happens to everyone at odds with himself—that is to say, to everyone at some point or other of his existence. As we have seen, something similar occurs in areas very different from illusion: the fantasy of the double is at work, for example, in the elementary mechanism of stupidity, but it is also present in a basic tendency of metaphysics or, at least, of a certain metaphysics.

Obviously, the fact that these various illusions share the theme of the double does not necessarily mean that every form of illusion is linked to the double. Before regarding such a conclusion as assured, we would have to carry out a complete inventory of all the manifestations of illusion, a feat which is, by definition, impossible. We shall simply note—following the example of barristers, who leave it to the prosecution to prove guilt—that the argument presented here remains true until such time as a case of illusion has been ranged against it that does not boil down, directly or indirectly, to a magical duplication and a confused hesitation between something unique and its double. A case which, it seems, still remains to be found.

Admittedly, we should perhaps have taken into account the famous 'illusions of the senses', which clearly bear no relation to the rejection of the real by duplication of it. But what are termed illusions of the senses are errors rather than illusions properly so called. Since they do not involve desire or fear—and it is difficult not to follow Freud on this point when, in *The Future of an Illusion* (1927), he links illusion, unlike error, to desire—they do not imply any protection from the real and may thus be equated with mere errors of judgement, as the Greek sceptics had already pointed out.

One would also have looked in vain for a means to contradict the thesis linking illusion to duplication in certain banal forms of illusion—those normally being referred to in everyday language when it says of such and such a person that 'they are deluded.' This 'being deluded' is said of common situations that may often seem far removed, admittedly, from the theme of the double. Thus I delude myself every day, each time I think of myself as intelligent, handsome, likeable, soon to be rich, soon to be showered with favours and honours. At first sight, this kind of banal illusion seems to lack any obvious relation to duplication. A more attentive examination would, however, show that in all cases the optimistic view of oneself and one's fate implies a chiasmus between what is perceived and what is deduced from the perception, which is analogous to the chiasmus involved in Boubouroche's distinguishing between the idea of his rival and the idea of the fidelity of his mistress. The character of Bélise in Molière's *Les Femmes savantes* (1672) is the typical example of this double vision that enables personal optimism to be reconciled with an ultimately realistic perception of the facts. Bélise believes she is beautiful, intelligent and loved; learning that Clitandre, whom she counts among her most attentive gallants, is about to marry a rival, she persuades herself all the more of Clitandre's feelings for her. We see the same attitude when it is pointed out that her other supposed lovers have all fled her presence:

nothing could be more normal, she replies, since they love me. Bélise manages at one and the same time to see that she is courted by no one and loved by everyone, just as Boubouroche saw simultaneously that Adèle had a lover and that she was faithful to him.

All illusory self-satisfaction—should that be all self-satisfaction?—ultimately involves this same duplicatory schema, which effects a paradoxical splitting between the thing and itself. The everyday blindness of self-perception, caricatured in the character of Bélise, is thus one variant among others of the fantasy of the double inherent in illusion. It is simply a derived, trivial form of the initial, 'noble' blindness we found in the oracle's curse and in tragedy. Its structure is not fundamentally different from that of all the illusions referred to above; one might venture to suggest that the same is probably the case with all illusion.

Lastly, It might be said to remain to show the presence of illusion—that is to say, of phantasmatic duplication—in most of the collective psychological investments of today and yesteryear—for example, in all forms of rejection or 'contestation' of the real, in which it is easy to establish that they could not succeed in indicting that which exists without the contribution of an ideal, unthinkable double. But there is a danger such a demonstration would take us into useless polemics and would lead, in the best of cases, only to the revelation of ultimately rather banal truths. It would be easy, but wearisome to develop the argument in this direction and I shall refrain from doing so here.